LO(

'Y LL

RAILWAYS OF NORTH WALES

GW 1498532 2

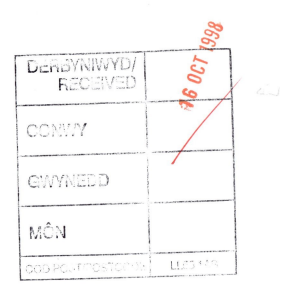

DERBYNIWYD/ RECEIVED	16 OCT 1998
CONWY	
GWYNEDD	
MÔN	
COB POUTHOSTEDIG	LLEG 440

RAILWAYS
of North Wales

by Walter Turner

Edited by Herbert Williams

JOHN JONES

Railways of North Wales
copyright Walter Turner, July 1998

First impression, July 1988

No part of this publication may be reproduced, stored in a retrieval stystem, or transmitted, in any form or by any means, electronic, mechanical, photocopying, recording or otherwise, without the permission of the publishers.
This book shall not, without the consent of the publishers, be lent, re-sold, hired out or otherwise disposed of by way of trade in any form of binding or cover other than that in which it was originally published.

ISBN 1 871083 11 7

Cover photographs by John Idris Jones and Walter Turner.
Text photographs by Walter Turner.

Printed and bound by MFP Design & Print, Thomas Street, Stretford, Manchester M32 0JT

Published by JOHN JONES PUBLISHING Ltd., Unit 12, Clwydfro Business Centre, Ruthin, North Wales, LL15 1NJ

CONTENTS

International Model Railway World
Kivoli Centre
Lein Amlwch Railway Centre
Llechwedd Slate Caverns
Llywernog Mine Museum
Mostyns Cafe
Penrhyn Castle Industrial Railway Museum

6.   Station Names and Other Attractions Map References

GENERAL INFORMATION

CLOSED LINES

The miniature railway at Eirias Park, Colwyn Bay closed at the end of 1996. The track was removed in spring 1997 to Gloddfa Ganol at Blaenau Ffestiniog.

The site at Gloddfa Ganol also closed in October 1997.

The 7¼ gauge line at Anglesey Bird World closed at the end of the 1997 season.

The railway at Butlin's Starcoast World closed in 1997 due to a landslide and is not expected to reopen.

Spring Hill Miniature Park at Devil's Bridge, opened in 1997 with a G gauge railway closed at the end of the season for relocation.

PROPOSED NEW LINES

It is proposed to build a 7¼ gauge line, which will be near Caernarfon.

The Llandudno Seaside Tramway Society proposes to restore an open top double-deck tramcar and operate it on a short line. For details contact the Membership Secretary, Llandudno Seaside Tramway Society, 12, Y Felin, Conwy. N. Wales LL32 8LW.

STANDARD GAUGE LINES

The Isle of Anglesey Railways Ltd is hoping to reopen the freight branch from Caerwen to Amlwch. For details write to Mr W.G. Davies, Brynthonfa, Ffordd Porth Llecog. AMLWCH. Ynys M n. LL68 9EA. Enclose your name and address, and a cheque or P.O. for £1.00 made payable to 'The Isle of Anglesey Railway Ltd'.

The Meirionnydd Railway Society is hoping to put passenger trains on the line from Blaenau Ffestiniog to Llan Ffestiniog and Trawsfynydd Lake Halt. For details contact the Membership Secretary, Mr Robert P Sheppard, 36 Muire Wood Drive, Curie, Edinburgh. EH14 5EZ.

The Llangollen Railway Society is going to extend the line from Carrog through to Corwen. Details from Llangollen Railway Society, The Station, Abbey Road, Llangollen, Denbighshire. LL20 8SN.

TICKETS

All stations are not manned and tickets may have to be bought on the train.

Combined tickets can be bought to cover more than one line. Check which restrictions apply before travelling.

RAIL ONLY

Coasts and Peaks, available 3 in 7 days or for 7 days. It covers the North Wales Coast from Holyhead to Crewe, including Llandudno and Blaenau Ffestiniog. Also Wrexham, Shrewsbury, Liverpool and Manchester, Stoke-on-Trent and Stafford.

There are Cambrian Coast Line Day and Evening Ranger Tickets between Pwllheli, Machynlleth and Aberystwyth.

Mid Wales Day Ranger Ticket, covering the lines from Shrewsbury to Chester, Telford, Machynlleth, Aberystwyth and Pwllheli.

Great Little Trains of Wales, available 4 days in 8 or for 8 days. Covering Bala Lake Railway, Brecon Mountain Railway, Ffestiniog Railway, Llanberis Lake Railway, Talyllyn Railway, Welsh Highland Railway Porthmadog, Welsh Highland Railway Caernarfon, Welshpool and Llanfair Railway, Vale of Rheidol Railway.

Ffestiniog Rover Ticket available 3 days in 7 or 7 days in 14. Covers the Ffestiniog Railway and the Welsh Highland Railway Caernarfon.

BUS AND RAIL TICKETS

The North and Mid Wales Rail Rover is available for 1 day, 3 days in 7 or for 7 consecutive days. This covers the main lines from Holyhead to Crewe. Shotton, and Chester to Wrexham and Shrewsbury. Crewe to Shrewsbury. Shrewsbury to Aberystwyth. Machynlleth to Pwllheli. It also covers the Ffestiniog Railway and buses in Gwynedd and Anglesey on services 1 to 99. Discounts are available to ticket holders on the Vale of Rheidol Railway, Welshpool and Llanfair Railway, and the Fairbourne and Barmouth Railway. Discounts are also available at some National Trust Properties.

There is also a Flexi Pass covering all Wales.

BUS TICKETS

Gwynedd Buses have a Red Rover Ticket for service numbers 1 to 99. It is available west of a line from Llandudno to Corwen, and north of Machynlleth.

Arriva Cymru (Crosville Cymru) has an Explorer ticket. This is run in conjunction with Stevensons and Midland Red. It is available on their services only. This covers North Wales from Chester to New Quay in the south. It is not available on service 701. Also on services to Manchester, Crewe, Shrewsbury and Birmingham. Some restrictions apply. There is also an Explorer Weekend Out Family Ticket available from 15.00 Friday to 09.00 Monday. Contact the bus companies for full details at any of their offices. Arriva Cymru, Head Office, Imperial Buildings, Glan-y-Mor Road, Llandudno Junction, Conwy C.B. LL31 9RU. Midland Red/Stevensons, Head Office, Delta Way, Cannock, Staffordshire, WS11 3WB.

DISABLED PASSENGERS

Some disabled toilets are fitted with the National Key System Locks. NKS keys can be bought from RADAR, 12 City Forum, 250 City Road, London EV1C 8AF.

It is advisable to contact the railway before travelling. The main companies covering the North Wales lines are: -

Holyhead to London direct: Virgin Trains, 85 Smallbrook, Queensway, Birmingham, B5 4HA.

North Wales Coast. Harwarden Bridge, Wrexham:

North Western Trains, P.O. Box 44, Rail House, Store Street, Manchester, M60 1DQ.

Chester, Chirk, Shrewsbury, Aberystwyth and Pwllheli:

Central Trains Ltd., Customer Services, P.O. Box 4323, Stanier House, 10 Holiday Street, Birmingham, B1 1TH.

1
STANDARD GAUGE LINES

NOTES ON STANDARD GAUGE LINES

The standard gauge is 4'-8 ⅜". The platforms are 3 feet above rail height but are allowed 1" tolerance. This normally gives a step up to the coach of 9". Should the platforms be below the standard height by more than 2" it has be noted in the station details. Basic stations consist of a platform with lights, no toilets or parking facilities. Should there be any difference to the above where possible a note has been made. Toilets and lifts at stations or in car parks are often closed after 19.00 hours and overnight. Most disabled toilets use the RADA key system.

Work is being done on upgrading station facilities and while this is going on some of them may be closed.

Radio Electric Token Block (RETB) now controls the lines from Shrewsbury to Machynlleth, Dovey Junction to Aberystwyth and Dovey Junction to Pwllheli.

The RETB is operated on these lines from the signal box at Machynlleth. When the driver wants to enter a section he will contact the signalman and ask for permission. If the section and the loop at the end are clear he will be given the radio token. The train will then proceed to the next crossing point. On entering the loop the driver will hand back the token to the signalman. (The token can then only be issued to a train going in the opposite direction.) After he has received the token for the next section he will proceed into it. Having cleared the loop he will inform the signalman by radio. Until he has done this, the signalman cannot issue the token for the section the train has left. There are however some short sections, which enable a second train to proceed into the section while the train is in the loop. These are not normally used.

At the loops there may be no signalman so the points are pre-set in the direction of travel. They are hydro-pneumatically operated and can be passed through in both directions. There is a speed restriction of 15 M.P.H. on the train. So that the driver approaching the points can see that they are pre-set correctly there is a yellow light on a marker board in advance of the points. This will only light when the points are pre-set correctly. The system of pre-set points is also used on other loops with signal boxes. Signals control the entry to the loop and are interlocked with the points.

Road crossings that are automatically controlled display a flashing red light to the driver. As the train approaches the crossing road lights operate, and the driver then sees a flashing white light.

CHESTER — HOLYHEAD

Lines from Birkenhead and Crewe had been opened to Chester in 1840 and the line from Chester via Saltney junction to Ruabon was opened in 1846. The Chester and Holyhead Railway opened the line from Saltney junction to Bangor in 1848. At the time only the up tube of the Conway Bridge was in use, the other tube being used from 1849. The line on Anglesey from Llanfair P.G. to Holyhead was opened in 1848. A new station was built in Holyhead in 1851. The Conway Tubular Bridge was 18 feet above high water and was the prototype for the Britannia Tubular Bridge across the Menai Strait, this bridge was opened in 1850. The L.N.W.R. took over the running of the line in 1859. The line became part of the L.M.S. and then the London Midland Region of British Railways.

From Chester you travel 2 miles to Saltney junction, here the line for Wrexham bears off to your left. You now pass over a road bridge with an industrial estate on the right, as you cross the bridge you come into Flintshire, Wales. After passing under a road bridge you will see the old engine shed at Mold junction. There used to be a station here called Saltney Ferry. On the left is Hawarden Airport. The river Dee is low down on your right, but you may not be able to see it. You then pass the site of the closed Sandycroft station. As you approach Queensferry you will see the bypass road bridge on the right and further down river the old Bascule Road Bridge. As you go over the old road you travel through the site of Queensferry station. On the right is the Bidston to Wrexham line, which you will pass under at Shotton Station. The station was closed in 1966 but the old platforms are still in place. It was reopened in 1972 with new platforms, which were built in place of the old slow lines. The steel works are on the opposite bank of the river.

2

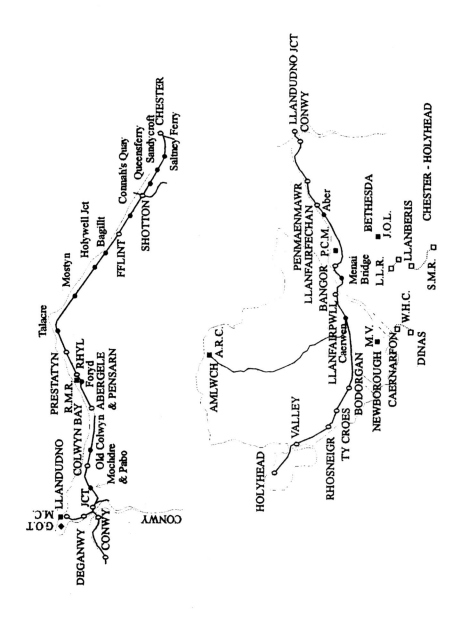

3

(Distances on the line are given from Chester)
For details of Shotton Station (8 Miles) see the Hawarden Bridge Wrexham line.

The next station was Connah's Quay. On the left you can see the old track bed of the Wrexham Mold and Connah's Quay railway. On the right is the site of the docks and you can see the new bridge crossing the river. The Dee now opens up into an estuary and the Wirral is on the other bank. The site of the old power station is just before you cross under the approach to the bridge. On the right is the new power station, which is supplied with gas from the Point of Ayr. You then go through the short Rockcliffe Hall tunnel (95yds). As you arrive at Fflint Station you can see the fire station on the left and on the right beyond the houses Fflint Castle.

FFLINT / FLINT
(12½ Miles)

Access to the platforms is on the side of the line going to Llandudno. There is a booking office, and waiting rooms on both platforms that are only open when the booking office is staffed. On the Llandudno side there are toilets for gentlemen and ladies, these may be locked but the key can be obtained from the booking office. To get to the Chester side platform you will need to cross the footbridge. There is a crossing at the Llandudno end of the platforms but staff must be available to see you across the lines. The station is near the town centre and shopping area.

How to Get There
At the junction of the A548 and A5119 there is a set of traffic lights. From the Connah's Quay direction, turn right. From Holywell direction turn left and from Northop carry straight on. The station car park is on the right.

The line continues along the coast with the A548 on the left. The station at Bagillt still has the platforms in place where the slow lines used to be. You pass Greenfield formerly the site of Holywell junction. The track bed of the line that went up to Holywell Town can be seen on the left and then some of the Station buildings. Look out on the right for the ship, The Duke of Lancaster, in the dry dock at Llannerch y mor. The line crosses the stream that goes by the dock on a short viaduct. In the car park on the left are some old buoys. Mostyn Dock is next on the

4

right. Some of the station buildings are still standing on the left. You will now travel along the sea wall.

On the right as you approach the Point of Ayr you can see the installation for bringing in gas from off shore. Beyond the sand dunes is the white lighthouse. The line now turns from a North Westerly direction to South Westerly. The platforms of Talacre station can be seen. After Talacre you go under a road bridge, by a caravan site. You go into Denbighshire before coming to Prestatyn. The station still has the old slow line platforms in place but only the centre island platform is used.

PRESTATYN
(26½ Miles)

On the platform is the booking office and waiting room. To get to it you have to cross a footbridge. The access is by a slope, which has 5" steps in it every 5'-6". There is a crossing over the line but the gates are locked and you would need staff to open them. There is a taxi rank and a telephone in the High Street near to the station. From the platform turn right over the footbridge and this leads to High Street, which is the main shopping centre. For the Bus station continue along High Street and turn right into Bridge Road. At the end you will see the Bus Station on the left across the road. The Tourist Information Office (summer only) is in the Offa's Dyke Centre Central Beach. From the platform turn left over the footbridge. When you come off the bridge turn left into Bastion Road, towards the traffic lights. Continue along Bastion Road to the sea front, the Offa's Dyke Centre is on the left.

How to Get There

Turn inland at the traffic lights on the A548, at the junction of Victory Road/ Marine Road with Bastion Road. At the end of Bastion road you will see a car park on your left and the footbridge on the right. From the A547 turn along Pendyffryn. After passing the Bus Station on your left, turn right into Bridge Road, then left into High Street. There is a car park on the left and the footbridge is at the end of High Street on the left.

As you leave the station you will see the signal box on the left and the track of the line that went to Dyserth. Soon you will see on the right the sky tower that is on the sea front at Rhyl. The station building on the right is listed grade 2 status.

5

RHYL
(30 Miles)

The station has two platforms. The one for the Llandudno direction can only be got to by the footbridge or the lift, which is only available when staff are at the station. The main entrance is on the Chester side from Station Square. The building has a booking office, waiting room and a telephone, there is also a telephone on the platform by the footbridge. When this entrance is closed there is a way onto the platform for Chester on the car park side of the building. On the Chester platform there are toilets for gentlemen, ladies and disabled. The Bus Station and Taxi rank are in Station Square. The Station is by the main shopping centre. The Tourist Information Centre is in the Children's Village, West Parade on the promenade. From the station go down the road opposite Bodfor Street and carry on along Queen Street until you come to the promenade, which is West Parade. The Children's Village is on your right. Other attractions are The Marine Lake and Miniature Railway, Ocean Beach Amusement Park, Sea Life Centre and Sun Centre.

How to Get There

Coming from Prestatyn, on the A548, follow the one way system in Rhyl and this will lead to the station*. From Abergele follow the A548 into the one way system and turn along High Street (A525 Rhuddlan). Turn right at the traffic lights and the station is on the right*. From Rhuddlan, on the A525, come over the railway bridge and turn left at the traffic lights, the station is on the left*.

* To get to the station car park carry on along this road (Kinmel Street) to the end and turn left into Elwy Street. The entrance to the car park is at the end on the left.

After leaving the station you will see on the right the Marine Lake with the miniature railway going round it. Crossing the river Clwyd on the Foryd viaduct you enter Conwy County Borough. On the left can be seen the course of the line that went to Denbigh. There was at one time a station at Kinmel Bay called Foryd. The line now goes under the A548 and heads for the coast. On the right are the new sea defences, which were remade after floods here at Towyn. The line now forms part of the sea wall.

6

ABERGELE & PENSARN
(Abergele, mouth of the river Gele. Pensarn, end of the paved way)
(34¼ Miles)

The station has two platforms. The one in the Llandudno direction is on a loop and is 2" too low. There is only a shelter on the Chester platform, that is 4" too low. To get between the platforms you will have to cross over by the railway bridge. Both platforms have access by a slope from the road. The station is due for improvement work.

How to Get There
The station is alongside Marine Road A548. From Abergele take the A458 in the Rhyl direction. When you come to the roundabout in Pensarn you will see the exit from it to the railway bridge. The station is on the right, where there is a small car park. To get to the Chester platform go over the railway bridge, turn right and first right to a small turning area by the platform.

From here the sea is on your right and the A55 expressway on your left. Beyond the road you can see Gwrych Castle, which is a modern structure. You go over the Llanddulas viaduct and pass the site of the station. On the right is a jetty for loading ships with stone from the quarry that is in the hill on the left. You will also see the viaducts of the A55, before you enter Penmaenrhos tunnel (485yds). Next comes the site of Old Colwyn station before crossing Colwyn and Groes viaducts and coming to Colwyn Bay station. The station has been rebuilt and the A55 goes under the forecourt of the station.

COLWYN BAY/ BAE COLWYN
(40½ Miles)

The station has two platforms. To get to the Chester platform, which has a waiting room, you will need to cross by the footbridge or lift. The Llandudno side is the main entrance in which there is a booking office and waiting room. It gives level access to the platform. The toilets are on the Llandudno platform for gentlemen, ladies and disabled. When the booking office is closed the entrance is on the left hand, car park side of the buildings. There is a taxi rank outside the station. The station is by the main shopping centre. The Tourist Information Centre is opposite the station in the building on the right of Station Road.

How to Get There

From the A547, coming from Abergele direction drive through the town centre and then turn right Hawarden Road. Turn right at the end into Princess Drive and the station will be on your left. From Mochdre follow the A547 across the roundabout to the traffic lights and turn left into Princes Drive. You will come to the station on your left. From the A55 Abergele direction come off at the Colwyn Bay exit turn right at the traffic lights and you will come to the station on your right. From the Llandudno direction you will not be allowed to turn left, therefore turn right. Follow the road, Victoria Avenue, to the mini roundabout. Go right round this and return the way you have just come. Carry straight on through the traffic lights and you will come to the station on your right. There are two entrances to the station car parks both long and short stay. The long stay is the one nearest Princess Drive end. Approach them with care.

The line now starts to bear left away from the sea and you will come to a section alongside the A55. Here there was a station called Mochdre and Pabo. Under the A55 is the site of the first water troughs in the world. They were built so that express trains did not have to stop to take on water. They were later moved to Aber further up the coast. The line of the present track is further north. On the left can be seen the Conwy Valley with the Castle on the other bank before the expressway blocks your view. The Conwy Valley line approaches on the left as you enter the junction. The original junction station of 1848 was to the west of the present station, which was opened in 1860.

LLANDUDNO JUNCTION
(44½ Miles)

To get to the station platform you must cross the footbridge or take the lift. There are call buttons for assistance on all the lift doors. The booking office and waiting room, which has a telephone, is on the main island platform. There is a bay platform 2 at the Llandudno end. The snack bar is between platforms 1 & 3. At the Rhyl end of platform 1 there is a toilet for gentlemen. The ladies is on platform 3. On the station forecourt there is also a telephone and a taxi rank.

How to Get There

The station is alongside the A547 Conwy Road. The entrance is on the Llandudno side where the road changes to Ferndale Road. Turn into the old part of Conwy road and left to the station. The long stay car park is on the right, and the short stay in front of the station.

Leaving the junction station you pass under the road bridge, look over on the left and you can see Conwy Castle and the bridges. On the right the line to Llandudno goes off, this was the site of the original station. The expressway carries straight on then goes under the river in a tunnel. As you cross over the Conwy you may just be able to see the Castle and road bridges on the right before you go into the Conwy Tubular Bridge (149yds). As you leave the Castle is on the right and you can see the old station goods yard with the hand crane still in place. Conwy station was closed in 1966 but reopened in 1987.

CONWY
(45½ Miles)

The station has two platforms with a shelter. To get to the Chester platform you go down the slope through the old car park at the corner of Lancaster Square. To get to the Bangor platform, cross over the railway bridge, Rosemary Lane. There are steps down to the platform on the right hand side of the bridge at the corner of Railway Terrace. To get to the platform by wheelchair is a long walk. From Lancaster Square go along the road in the Llandudno direction, this is Rose Hill Street. You will see a path on the left, which goes through the town walls. Follow it and go under the railway. On the other side turn right and follow the lane back until you come to the station on your right. Lancaster Square is in the shopping area. Walk along Rose Hill Street and you will come to The Visitor Centre. Further along on the right there is a car park. At the end is the entrance to the Castle and The Tourist Information Centre where there are toilets for gentlemen, ladies, and disabled. The other attractions in Conwy include Teapot World museum and shop in Castle Street. Butterfly Jungle, Bodlondeb Park and the Smallest House on The Quay.

How to Get There

From Llandudno direction follow the A547 through the one way system and you will come to the station on your right. From the Bangor direction, on the A547, you follow the one way system right through the town and at the roundabout turn back toward Bangor and join the way from Llandudno. There is no parking at the station. To get to the nearest car park from the roundabout take the road by the side of the Castle, B5106 Llanrwst Road. You will come to a car park on your right. From the car park to get to the Bangor platform take the lane on the left of the foot tunnel entrance. For the Chester platform go under the tunnel and follow the path, this will bring you out in Rose Hill Street. Carry straight on and the station is on your left.

After the station you enter Conwy tunnel (74yds), and cross under the express way. On the right you can see the Great Orme across Conwy Bay. You will follow the expressway on your left before entering the Penmaenbach tunnel (718yds), which is on a curve. As you entered the tunnel you came into the Snowdonia National Park and as you leave the tunnel you have already left the park. This is the only time the coastline is within the park so you could say it does not travel in the park but under it. The expressway is on the left and if you look out on the right you will see the tip of Ynys Mon / Anglesey. On the tip is the Black and White lighthouse and to the right Perch Rock lighthouse and then Puffin Island or Priestholm. You next enter the Moel Llys tunnel (154yds), and as you leave the expressway is on the right.

At Penmaenmawr you will see on the right the sidings for the stone quarry which is in the hill on the left.

PENMAENMAWR
(Top of the large stone)
(49¾ Miles)

The station has two platforms. To get to the Chester side you will have to cross a footbridge. The platform has a shelter and is 3" too low. The Bangor platform has level access from the road. There is a telephone outside the station entrance and the nearest toilets for gentlemen ladies and disabled are across the road in the car park.

How to Get There

From the old main road at the junction of Bangor Road/Ffordd Bangor, Fernbook Road and Pent yr Afon go down Paradise Road. The station is at the junction at the bottom with Station Road West and Station Road East. The car park is on the right.

After crossing under the expressway you enter the Pen y Clip tunnel (265yds) part of which is an avalanche tunnel. The original road tunnel is above you. As you leave the tunnel the line crosses the Penmaenmawr viaduct.

LLANFAIRFECHAN
(52¼ Miles)

The station has two platforms joined by a footbridge. The Bangor platform is 5" too low and has a shelter. There is a footpath to it, up a slope from Station Road. The Chester platform has a shelter and is 3" too low, it has access from the car park up a slope. The nearest telephone and toilets for gentlemen ladies and disabled are in the beach car park. From the station go to Station Road and turn left, the car park is along the road.

How to Get There
From the traffic lights on the old main road in the centre of the town, go down Station Road. When you come to the expressway bridge there is a footpath on the left for the Bangor platform. For the Chester platform carry on under this bridge and the railway bridge. A footpath on the left leads to the car park. In a car carry on and take first left along West Shore, this will lead you to the car park by the station.

The expressway swings inland and as you cross a small stream you enter Gwynedd. The line continues along the entrance to the Menai Strait. On the right is a nature reserve and Beaumaris can be seen on Anglesey. On the left is the village of Abergwyngregyn. This is where the water troughs were moved to from Mochdre and the station of Aber. You can see Penrhyn Castle on the right before you go over Llandegai viaduct (over the Afon Ogwen) and through Llandegai tunnel (505yds). There is an industrial estate on the right before crossing the Gegin viaduct over the Afon Gegin. The narrow gauge line from the Penrhyn Quarry at Bethesda passed under this viaduct on its way to Porth Penrhyn. The course of the standard gauge line from Bethesda can be seen on the left as you leave the viaduct, before you enter Bangor tunnel (890yds). At the station, on the left, is the old locomotive shed, now in private use. The other end of the yard is still used by the railway.

BANGOR
(59¾ Miles)

There are two island platforms but only one side of each is used. The main building has a booking office with a footbridge to both platforms. There is a lift to platform 2, which has a shelter. Access to platform 1 is by a slope from behind the main building. Trains can leave from both platforms in either direction. On

Platform 1 there is a telephone, buffet and waiting room, also toilets for gentlemen, ladies, and disabled. There is a taxi rank outside the main building. Bangor has a shopping centre. From the station turn right at the traffic lights along Station Road and turn left into High Street. As you continue along High Street you will come to the shops. For the Tourist Information Centre (Summer only) leave the station and go straight across the road at the traffic lights and along Deiniol Road. Walk along for ½ mile and you will see a white building on your right, just before the post office. This is the Town Hall and the centre is in here, at the far end.

How to Get There

From the A55 take the A5122 into Bangor. Follow this road, until you come to a set of traffic lights and the Station is in front of you. From Caernarfon direction on the A4082 you will go under the railway bridge and have to turn left. The station entrance is on the left at the traffic lights. From Menai Bridge direction follow the A5122 until you come to the traffic lights by the station, there is no right turn so you will have to turn left into Deiniol Road, first right into Farrar Road, continue to the end and turn right into High Street. Then first right into Station Road. The entrance is on your left at the traffic lights. As you enter the station the car park is on your left. There is a one way system round the main station building.

As the train leaves the station you enter Belmont tunnel (648yds), which is built on a curve. Leaving it you see the Menai Strait on the right and looking forward on this side you can see the Suspension Bridge and further away the Britannia Bridge. After going under the A487 you will see the site of Menai Bridge station. This was the junction for the line to Caernarfon, the course of it can be seen further along on the left. When it was built it had the distinction of being named after the town in the next county and across a bridge. There was a station originally at the entrance to the bridge, called Britannia Bridge but this was closed when Menai Bridge opened.

The Britannia Bridge was closed in May 1970 due to a fire. It was rebuilt as an open bridge. The towers were raised to accommodate the A5 road, which now is above the railway line. It was reopened to rail traffic in January 1972. The line now uses the left side over the bridge, which is a single track, but room has been left to double the track should it be required. You get good views along the strait, which was

12

not possible when it was a tubular bridge. On the right is the Suspension bridge and on the left are views towards Caernarfon. The supergrid electric line you see alongside are the 400 thousand volt lines from Pentir Substation, near Bangor, to the substation at Wylfa Nuclear Power Station. As you cross over the bridge you enter Ynys Mon / Anglesey. Leaving the bridge the track once more becomes double. Should you look back on the right you may just see the column that was erected in 1860 to the First Marquess of Anglesey

LLANFAIR-PWLL-GWYNGYLL-GOGERYCHWYRN-DROBWLL-LLANTYSILIO-GOGOGOCH
(St. Mary's church-in the hollow-white hazels-near to the rapid whirlpool-St. Tysil's church-red cave)
(63½ Miles)
The official name of the village is Llanfair Pwllgwyngyll, but you will find the bus etc carry the signs Llanfair P.G. The station was closed in 1966 but reopened when the Britannia Bridge was closed in 1970 due to the fire. The station has two platforms with a shelter on the Holyhead side. A footbridge connects the platforms. The station buildings, adjacent car park and large shop belong to James Pringle Weavers. The shop is worth a visit and has a restaurant. In the shop are two 15" gauge locomotives that used to run on the marine lake railway at Rhyl. Railway Queen and Michael are both 4-4-2. The Tourist Information Centre is on the left as you enter the shop.

How to Get There
The station is alongside the main road in the village, Holyhead Road. Coming from Bangor on the A5, cross the Menai Straits on the Britannia Bridge. Take the first exit left, and turn left onto the A4080 heading to Llanfairpwllgwyngyll. As you leave the slip road you enter Llanfairpwllgwyngyll, this is the old A5 road. Keep straight on until you come to the station on your left. The car park belongs to the shop and is locked when the shop is closed. There is a footpath open at all times to the platform. Should you need to get to the Holyhead platform without going over the footbridge, follow the road back toward Bangor until you pass the pedestrian crossing, turn right along the lane and go across the level crossing. Turn right along the path to the platform. Note the level crossing gates are both on one side when they are open for road traffic.

Looking over to the left as the train proceeds you may be able to see Snowdon. 2¾ miles from Llanfair P.G. is Gaerwen junction. This is where the line to Amlwch goes off to the right. Part of the earthworks for the station platforms can be seen. The line now enters a series of cuttings before emerging across Malltraeth Marsh or Cors Ddyga. On the far side you cross Bogorgan viaduct over the Afon Cefniand and the drainage channels. There are now the only tunnels on the island, Bodorgan No 1 (413yds) and No 2 (115yds).

BODORGAN
(72½ Miles)
This is a request stop with two platforms. The Bangor side is 6" too low. To get to the other side you will have to you use the foot crossing. The Holyhead side is 3" too low and has a shelter.

How to Get There
There are two villages nearby. From Bethel take the minor road for Llangadwaladr, when the road turns left over the railway bridge carry straight on. The station is on the left. From Llangadwaladr take the minor road to Bethel. After going over the railway bridge turn left and the station is on the left.

You now pass Llyn Coron on the left before coming to Ty Croes.

TY CROES
(Cross House)
(75¼ Miles)
This is a request stop. There are two platforms. The Bangor platform is on the Bangor side of the level crossing and is 15" too low. The Holyhead platform is on that side of the crossing. They both have a slope up and have shelters.

How to Get There
The nearest village is Bryn Du. From the centre of the village, take the road east and the station is ¼ mile on the left.

On the left is Llyn Maelog and two old windmills are on the right.

RHOSNEIGR
(77 Miles)
This is a request stop. The two platforms each have a shelter. They each have an approach up a slope from the road that goes

Virgin Trains HST at Rhosneigr with the 13.35 Sundays only from Holyhead, bound for London on the Chester – Holyhead route.

under the railway bridge. Both platforms are 5" too low.

How to Get There

From the centre of the village go north along the A4080 Station Road. The station is ¼ mile on the right hand side of the A4080 by the railway bridge.

After crossing Trewin Sands viaduct you will see the golf course on the left then Valley Airfield. Should you notice the train passing signals that are not lit do not worry. These are there in case the airfield blocks the line when the control tower can set them at red to warn the trains of danger. Before you get to Valley Station on the right is the freight siding where the flasks from Wylfa Nuclear Power station are loaded onto the rail. The triangle is also here for turning steam engines round when they come to Holyhead. You now come to Valley Station, which was closed in 1966 and reopened in 1982.

VALLEY/Y DYFFRYN
(81 Miles)

This is a request stop. The Holyhead side is approached from the level crossing up a slope and has a shelter. On the Bangor side there is a slope from the small car park. The platform is 12" too low and the only protection is the overhang of the old station buildings.

How to Get There
From the junction of the A5 and A5025 take the B4545 Trearddur road. You will come to the level crossing. The small car park is on the right before the crossing.

Holyhead is on an island and on the left can be seen part of the sea that surrounds it. You now cross the Stanley Embankment, the road is the other side of the wall on your right. Part way across there is an opening in the embankment with gates. You are now on Holyhead Island/Ynys Gybi. After leaving the embankment the Aluminium Works is on the right. Shortly you enter Holyhead. The train servicing area is on the right and on the left old cattle docks and carriage shed.

HOLYHEAD / CAERGYBI
(84½ Miles)

The station is the end of the line and is at the end of the docks. The old entrance was down a slope that leads to the building between platforms 1 & 2, in which there is a waiting area and toilets. New facilities and the main booking office are at the sea end of platforms 2 & 3. Go onto platform 2 and turn left, here there is a cafe and at the end the new main building. Platform 2 is 8" too low. You are able to walk between all the platforms to the new building by a slope or on the level. The new buildings contain booking offices for the railway and shipping lines, a waiting room, telephones, Tourist Information Centre, also toilets for gentlemen, ladies and disabled.

How to Get There
As you enter Holyhead on the A5 you will come to a set of traffic lights. For the new entrance carry straight on and you will see the station on your left. There is also long stay parking in this area, follow the signs. There is no overnight parking allowed on the station car park. To get to the car park turn left at the lights, go over the bridge, past the old entrance on your right. Continue down the road on the other side. At the end of the slope you join the B4545 and the car park entrance is on the right. A footbridge with a lift connects the car park with the station waiting area, between platforms 1 & 2 in the old building.

16

SHREWSBURY — ABERYSTWYTH

Between 1859 and 1864 the line was opened in sections by several companies. The Shrewsbury and Welshpool Branch Railway built the section from Sutton Bridge Junction, Shrewsbury to Hanwood (with a branch to Minsterley), in 1861, extending to Buttington junction in 1862. This line was operated by the L.N.W.R. with through traffic for the G.W.R. It became a joint G.W.R. & L.M.S line. From Buttington Junction the line was part of the Oswestry and Newtown Railway. It opened to Welshpool in 1860 and to Newtown in 1861. The section from Newtown to Moat Lane Junction was opened in 1859 as part of the Llanidloes and Newtown Railway. The Newtown and Machynlleth Railway built the line from Moat Lane Junction, which was opened in 1863. The Aberystwith and Welch Coast Railway opened from Machynlleth to Borth in 1863 and on to Aberystwyth in 1864. The lines from Buttington Junction to Aberystwyth became part of the Cambrian Railways, and then became part of the G.W.R. In British Railways time all the lines were part of the Western Region until 1963 when they became part of the London Midland Region.

Leaving Shrewsbury you will see a radio mast on the right. This is because Radio Electronic Token Block, controlled from the signal box at Machynlleth, operates the line from here to Machynlleth. The train will stop at Sutton Bridge Junction. The driver will contact Machynlleth by radio to pick up the radio token for the single line to Welshpool, which is first station on the line in Wales. You will now travel 13 miles before you cross into Wales near Middletown, Powys. The boundary is a small stream between two cuttings. At this point there are hills on both sides of you. The hill on the right side has a quarry scar on it. The A458 road crosses over the line and you enter the Severn Valley.

You can see the old track bed from Oswestry coming in on the right. Then you will pass the closed station of Buttington Junction. At this point the mileage of the line changes from miles from Sutton Bridge Junction to miles from Whitchurch by Oswestry. The line used to be double track from here to Welshpool. On the other side of the valley is the A483, the main road from Oswestry, and the Shropshire Union Canal. The train

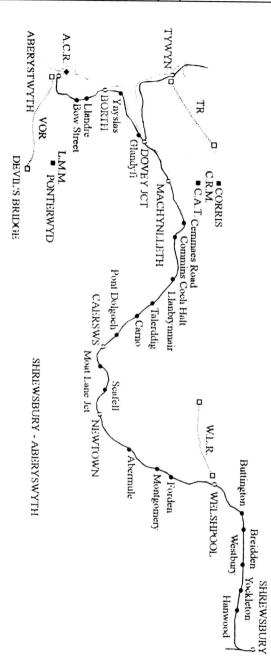

SHREWSBURY - ABERYSTWYTH

crosses over the short Buttington Gates Flood viaduct (38yds) then goes over the site of Offa's Dyke just before the level crossing. You cross the river Severn and the train runs alongside the A483 bypass as you enter Welshpool's new station.

(Distances for the line are given from Shrewsbury)

WELSHPOOL / Y TRALLWNG
(19¾ Miles)

The station is a passing point on the line and the radio tokens will be exchanged here. It consists of an island platform with a shelter. The new platform was built when the road by-pass was constructed along the old track bed. Access is by a ramped footbridge. There is a small car park at the side of the old station. The old station has now been converted into a shop and cafe. You can sit in the cafe, which is on the old platform, and watch the cars go by and occasionally the train.

Attractions in the town are The Welshpool and Llanfair Railway, Raven Square, Powisland Museum and Canal Centre in Severn Street, Powis Castle and Deer Park. The Tourist Information Centre is in Vicarage Gardens Car Park, Church Street. From the station cross over the footbridge to the car park by the old station buildings, opposite is Severn Street, walk along it to the traffic lights, Church Street is on the right.

How to Get There

The station is alongside the A483. At the roundabout by the station take the road for Welshpool B4381. Immediately there is a second roundabout and the car park is off this roundabout on the left.

Leaving you will see a small nature reserve on the left and Powis Castle is on the hill on the right. You continue to run alongside the bypass and then the road goes off to the right. The line crosses a short viaduct Glanhafron (31yds) and the Cilcewydd (74yds) crossing over the Severn. On the opposite side is the Welshpool Mid Wales Airport then the A483 main road and beyond it the canal. As you follow the valley you will pass the sites of three closed stations that were all passing points. At Forden you can see the old station buildings and signal box on the right with the yard on the left. At Montgomery the remains of the platform are on the right, the yard and goods shed on the left. Abermule has the station buildings and platform on your right and the yard on the left. As you enter Newtown you will pass industrial estates on both sides of the line.

NEWTOWN/Y DRENEWYDD
(33¾ Miles)

The station is a passing point on the line and the radio tokens will be exchanged here. The station buildings are occupied, with a taxi firm using part of the building on the Welshpool side. Both platforms have a shelter, and are connected by a footbridge. On the platform for Welshpool there is a slope and the old section at the Machynlleth end is 8" too low. There is only a small car parking area by the station. The Tourist Information Centre is at The Park, Back Lane. To get there from the Welshpool side of the station, turn right and walk to Old Kerry Road. Turn left along it to the main road. Cross into Short Bridge Street, which will lead you into the shopping area. Continue into Broad Street and turn left into Wesley Street. You will see the centre on your left on the corner of Wesley Street and Back Lane.

How to Get There

Take the A483 in the Welshpool direction and turn right into the A489 Kerry Road. Turn right into Old Kerry Road, follow the road keeping to the left at the fork junction. The station is on your left in Station Yard. To get to the Machynlleth platform after the fork junction turn left into Brimmon Lane, cross over the railway bridge, and there is a slope down to the platform on your right.

Leaving Newtown you will notice how long the loop is before the line becomes single track. The line crosses over two main roads, the A483 and A489, before crossing over the Severn. You then pass the site of Scafell Halt. The line from Newtown to Moat Lane Junction was at one time doubled but a second platform was never built at the Halt. Crossing the river for a second time on Doughty's viaduct (62yds), before going under the A489, the train continues to turn left then enters a straight section. As it swings to the right you will see the closed Moat Lane Junction platforms on the left. The old line to Llanidloes and Builth Wells goes straight on. After the main road level crossing you will go over a viaduct (66yds) and cross the River Severn for the last time before entering Caersws. There was a Roman Fort here and the station is on the site of the baths.

20

CAERSWS
(39¼ Miles)
There is only a single platform, which is 5" too low with a signal box at the level crossing end.

How to Get There
Take the B4569 heading south and you will come to the station. Across the level crossing on the right cars may be parked in the old goods yard.

Leaving you will see the A470 road on your right and the Afon Carno on the left. As the line crosses over the main road the buildings of closed Pontdolgoch station are on the left. The road keeps to the left of the valley but the line crosses over the river several times. As you pass Carno on your left look up to the skyline over the village and you will see the wind turbines for generating electricity. Next you will see the old station buildings on the left and go over the level crossing. The train starts to leave the valley and climbs up to the crossing point at Talerddig that is 693 feet above sea level. There is a house on the site of the former station. The radio mast is on the left and the driver will exchange the radio electric token before proceeding to Machynlleth.

Leaving the loop you go through a cutting that is 120ft deep. This was the deepest railway cutting in the world when it was made. Up to now all the rivers you have seen have flowed into the Severn, they now flow into the Dyfi. As the train crosses the main road look out on the left and you will get a nice view down the valley. The train goes down the valley following the Afon Iaen. Passing the site of Llanbrynmair the old station building is on the left, the platform was cut in two by the level crossing. You now follow the Afon Twymyn, passing Commins Coch where there used to be a halt and on to Cemmaes Road. As you swing left you will see the Dyfi valley on your right and then go under the road bridge into the old station site. This was the junction with the line to Dinas Mawddwy and on the right you can just make out where the track ran. A radio mast is on the right in the old goods yard. The train now follows the wide valley of the River Dovey / Afon Dyfi to Machynlleth. Look over on your right and you will see the electric wind turbine of the Centre of Alternative Technology, which is in the valley where the Corris Railway ran.

Machynlleth station. 150131 (left) with the 14.00 going to Shrewsbury, with 153333 awaiting the next trip to Pwllheli along the Cambrian Coast line.

MACHYNLLETH
(The field of Cynllaith)
(61 Miles)

This is now the main station for changing trains for the Cambrian Coast line to Pwllheli. At the Shrewsbury end of the station on the right is the signal box that controls the radio tokens for all the lines from Machynlleth. Signals, both semaphore and electric light, control the station and the section to Dovey Junction. The station has two platforms and a passing loop, also sidings and a goods yard. There is a waiting room and booking office on the side for Aberystwyth and Pwllheli. The toilets for gentlemen, ladies and disabled are on the Shrewsbury side of the main building. They may be locked, but a key can be obtained from the station staff. The platform for Shrewsbury is connected by a footbridge and has a shelter. From this platform there is also a slope down to the main road that can be used by wheelchairs.

There is a shopping centre in the town. Leave the station and at the main road turn left. Follow the road for ¼ mile and you are in the town centre. For the Tourist Information Centre follow the road to the clock tower and turn left into Maengwyn Street and the centre is along on the left in the Canolfan Owain Glyndwr.

How to Get There
From the town centre take the A487 Dolgellau road. The station approach is on the right opposite the bus depot. There is a coach and car park. For wheelchair access to Shrewsbury platform carry on under the railway bridge and there is a slope on the right.

Coming on the A493 from Aberdyfi or the A487 from Dolgellau at the junction turn over the river bridge for Machynlleth on the A487. After passing under the railway bridge take first left into the station approach.

As the train leaves Machynlleth the trains for Pwllheli and Aberystwyth use the same single line to Dovey Junction. The line is controlled by colour light signals from the Machynlleth signal box. You will see the afon Dyfi meandering on your right and the A487 road on your left. 2¼ miles from Machynlleth the line passes into Gwynedd and the Snowdonia National Park for ¼ mile before returning into Powys. At the junction the Aberystwyth train will take the left hand line and the Pwllheli train will use the right hand line.

DOVEY JUNCTION / CYFF DYFI
(65 Miles)
The station is the junction where the Aberystwyth and Pwllheli trains take their own lines and the train picks up the electric token for their respective line. This was a main interchange point on the line. Today connections are timed so that they can be made at Machynlleth. The only access, except by rail, is by a track from the end of the Aberystwyth platform. Cross over the line to the walkway beside the railway bridge over a stream, then follow the rough track to Glandyfi.

The train will cross from Powys into Ceredigion as you cross over the stream outside the station. At Glandyfi you can see on the left the old station and the yard that is now a private garden. The line now bears right crossing over Cottage Pie viaduct (24yds) and keeps to the south bank of the Dyfi estuary. Looking across you will be able to see the white houses of Aberdyfi. Part way along you cross the Trer'ddol viaduct (28yds). As the train swings to the left you will come to the site of Ynys Las station. Notice the old railway carriage on the left and the radio mast. After going over the level crossing you cross the Afon Leri on a viaduct (49yds). The train now heads south along the coast. The B4353 road is on the right and the sea wall beyond. Looking to your left and slightly forward you will see in the hills another site with wind turbines for electric generation. You can see these more clearly as you get nearer Aberystwyth.

BORTH
(Harbour)
(73¾ Miles)

The station is a single platform with a shelter. This is a short section working for the radio tokens.

How to Get There
From the High Street, B4353, which is the promenade. Go along Cambrian Terrace. On the corner is the Tourist Information Centre (only open in summer). The station is at the end of the road with car parking spaces on the left.

From Borth your train will have to climb up to Bow Street station to get over to the Rheidol valley. You will pass the site of Llandre station, on the right where there is a modern house and on the left the old goods yard. At Bow Street the station yard can be seen on the left.

The line now drops down to the Rheidol. It crosses the A487 road, goes under two minor roads and runs alongside the A44 road before crossing it. You will see the Rheidol and the narrow gauge Vale of Rheidol line on your left. It crosses over the river on a bridge and the two lines now start to come closer to each other. Each goes over the A4120 road on their own level crossing. The radio mast is on your left, and you will also see the sheds of the narrow gauge line.

ABERYSTWYTH
(81½ Miles)

This is the end of the line and the radio token point. The station has recently been refurbished, and now has only one platform. On it there is a booking office, buffet and toilets for gentlemen, ladies and disabled. The entrance is at the side of the station. When you get off the train, turn right and at the end of the platform there is a ramp from the platform down to road level.

24

There is a small car park at the side but plenty of parking in the area. For the Vale of Rheidol line turn left on the platform. You will see booking office and shop for the railway at the end of the station buildings.

The Aberystwyth cliff railway is at the end of the promenade. For the Tourist Information Centre go across Ffordd Alexandra/Alexandra Road into Ffordd y Mor/Terrace Road and the centre is on the right hand side near the sea front.

How to Get There
Coming by bus you will get off on the north side of the station. Walk along Ffordd Alexandra/Alexandra Road in the direction of the traffic, past the front of the station, turn left and the ramped entrance is on your left.

By road from the north on the A487 follow the one way system and you will be directed past the station along Ffordd Alexandra/Alexandra Road. Continue to the roundabout and turn left into Coedlan y Parc/Park Avenue. You will find plenty of car parks along this road.

From the south on the A487, after crossing the Rheidol Bridge turn first right into Dan Dre/Mill Street. At the roundabout turn right into Coedlan y Parc/Park Avenue. You will find plenty of car parks along this road.

MACHYNLLETH — PWLLHELI

The line was started by The Aberystwith and Welch Coast Railway, which had built the line from Machynlleth to Borth in 1863 and to Aberystwyth in 1864. Their intention was to build a bridge across the river from Ynys Las to Aberdyfi. The line from Aberdyfi to Llwyngwril opened in 1863 and to Barmouth Junction with the terminus at Penmaenpool in 1865. The railway had plans to continue to Pwllheli and with a junction at Afon Wen to the line from Caernarfon. In 1865 the railway became part of the Cambrian Railways who continued with the plans, opening up the line to Pwllheli in 1867. Before a proposed bridge had been built from Ynys Las to Aberdyfi a ferry service operated across the river. It was found it was not possible to bridge the estuary at this point so the line from Aberdyfi had to be extended along the north shore of the estuary. The line was taken through tunnels round the back of Aberdyfi to bridge across the

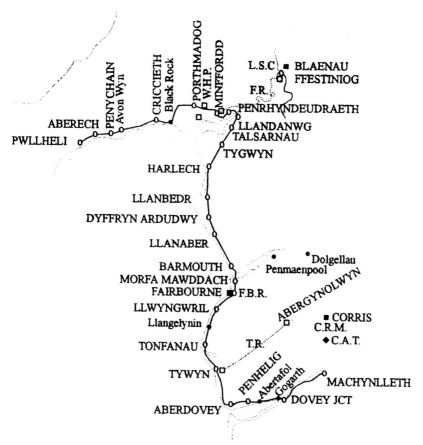

MACHYNLLETH - PWLLHELI

Dyfi nearer Machynlleth. The line was opened in 1867 to a new junction, which today is Dovey Junction/Cyff Dyfi. (At first it was called Glandovey then Morben then Dovey Junction.) The bridge across the river originally had an opening span to let shipping through. It was rebuilt about 1914 without it. The Cambrian also extended the line from Penmaenpool to Dolgelley / Dolgellau in 1869. The line became part of the G.W.R., then Western Region of British Railways, and London Midland Region in 1963.

As the train leaves Machynlleth it is in Powys. The trains for Pwllheli and Aberystwyth use the same single line to Dovey

Junction. The line is controlled by colour light signals from the Machynlleth signal box. You will see the Afon Dyfi meandering on your right and the main road on your left. 2¼ miles from Machynlleth the line passes into Gwynedd and the Snowdonia National Park, for ¼ mile before returning into Powys. At the junction the Aberystwyth train will take the left hand line and the Pwllheli train will use the right hand line.

(The distances on the line are from Machynlleth)

For details of Dovey Junction (4 Miles) see Shrewsbury - Aberystwyth line

Leaving the junction the train crosses the river Dyfi on the Dovey Junction Viaduct (152yds) and heads for the north shore of the estuary. You now re-enter Gwynedd and the Snowdonia National Park. As the line turns west along the shore you will see the A493 road to Tywyn on your right. The line comes close to the road and this is the area of the old Gogarth Halt. The train will now continue along the side of the estuary. There are high cliffs above you on the right. There are now four tunnels on the line called Aberdovey number 1 to 4. No 1 is 200yds long, and then in ¾ mile you enter No 2 tunnel that is 219yds long. As you leave you pass the site of the old Abertafol Halt. 1¼ miles on you enter No 3 tunnel that is 191yds long, The main road crosses over the top of the tunnel to the estuary side of the line. As you leave the tunnel you will cross the main road and enter Penhelig station.

PENHELYG / PENHELIG
(9 Miles)

The station was classified as a halt and is a request stop and has a single platform 8" too low with a shelter. It is on the inland side of the line and the only access is by steps up from the main road on the Aberdyfi side of the station.

How to Get There

The station is alongside the A493. From both directions the road comes under a railway bridge. On the inland side of the road is a car park. Be careful of the small one way system to the car park.

Leaving the station the line crosses over the road and enters tunnel No 4 Craig-y-Don, that is the longest at 533yds. You leave it at the back of Aberdyfi and the line will shortly cross over the main road once more to the side of the estuary and will come to Aberdyfi station.

ABERDYFI / ABERDOVEY
(The mouth of the river Dovey)
(10 Miles)

The station has only one platform on the inland side of the line. It has a shelter. The platform is 12" too low but a set of portable steps are on the platform. This used to be a passing point on the line. For the nearest toilets go to main road, turn right and walk towards Aberdyfi and then down the lane on your left by the Neuadd Dyfi.

The Tourist Information Centre (summer only) is on the sea side of The Wharf Gardens, which are in the main street.

How to Get There

The station is on the outskirts of Aberdyfi. Take the A493 from the town centre toward Tywyn. Go under the railway bridge, and after you have passed a petrol station on the right hand side with the bus stop opposite, take first left. The station is at the end of this road on the right. There is a small car park. The platform has level access from the car park.

Leaving you will see the golf course on your left. The train now starts to head north and you will see the Coastguard lookout post on the right. The main road runs by the railway most of the way to Tywyn. Going under a small footbridge you leave the Snowdonia National Park. As you enter Tywyn you will see on the right the Talyllyn Railway's Wharf station.

TYWYN
(Sand Dunes)
(13½ Miles)

The station is a passing point on the line and here the radio tokens will be exchanged.

There are shelters on both platforms and these are 9" too low. There is level access to the Pwllheli platform and a slope up to the Machynlleth platforms from the car park. The nearest toilets are at the side of the car park, and there is also a telephone by the main road. The station is by the shopping centre, and just a short walk away is the Talyllyn Wharf Station. The Tourist Information Centre (summer only) is in High Street on the right hand side. From the station car park, High Street is opposite on the left.

How to Get There
The station is alongside the A493. There is a car park, which is locked from 21.00 to 07.00 each night. To get to the Pwllheli platform you will have to go under the railway bridge and you will see the entrance on your left

Leaving Tywyn the line goes towards the sea and you will soon be running alongside the sea wall. There is a road on the right. When it comes to the Dysynni you will see there is no bridge, but the road continues on the other side of the river. You again re-enter the Snowdonia National Park and soon your train arrives at Tonfanau.

TONFANAU
(16 Miles)
The station is a request stop. There is only a small platform on the sea side of the line, with a shelter. The station has no lighting, so trains do not stop here early morning or evening.

How to Get There
The station is alongside a minor road near the south end of the village. There is a small area opposite where cars could be parked.

The next stage of the line runs along the edge of the coast and you will see the A493 road appear on your right. ¾ mile further on you will see a chapel on the right. This was the area of the now closed Llangelynin Halt. The next station is Llwyngwril.

LLWYNGWRIL
(20 Miles)
The station is a request stop. It was an old passing point on the line. The platform is on the inland side of the line and has a shelter. It is 10" too low and a set of steps is available.

How to Get There
From the centre of the village on the A483 by the bridge over the stream, go down Ffordd Yr Orsaf (Station Road). The station is under ¼ mile on the left. There is a small car park.

The train now starts to climb up to the cliff with the sea on your left. (This is the sea end of the Cader Idris Range.) Near the top there is a 15

29

M.P.H. speed limit for the train. You will pass through an open shelter, which is there to protect the line from any rock falls. It was built in 1933. You will notice the reinforcement that has taken place on the cliff faces. At Friog you are at the top of the line, 100 feet above the sea. The road is 100 feet above you. From the top of the climb the line runs down hill to Fairbourne. As the line swings inland you will see on the left the sea wall still has the anti tank landing concrete blocks in place. These are known locally as dragon's teeth. The road is on your right and this is the boundary of the Snowdonia National Park. Just before entering Fairbourne station you will see the coach sheds and station of the Fairbourne Miniature Railway.

FAIRBOURNE
(22¾ Miles)
The station is a single platform on the sea side of the railway. The platform has a shelter and is 3" too low. The station is across the road from the Fairbourne Miniature Railway. There are shops and cafes nearby.

How to Get There
From the A493 take the road to Fairbourne, after going over the level crossing turn right for the station and car park. There is a ramp to access the platform. Toilets are next to the road.
The line continues to Morfa Mawddach.

MORFA MAWDDACH
(23¾ Miles)
This station was known as Barmouth Junction. The Cambrian line joined with a line that ran from here to Dolgellau. It has been made into a cycle track and footpath for most of the way called Llwybr Mawddach Trail. The platform, which is on the inland side of the line, has a shelter and level access from the car park. At the end of the old Dolgellau platform there are toilets for gentlemen, ladies and disabled. You can walk over the toll bridge alongside the railway line to Barmouth.

How to Get There
The road to the station leads off the A493. It is 1 mile north of the Fairbourne turn off and 1¼ miles south of Arthog. The station and car park are at the end of the road.

You now swing towards Barmouth. The first part of the line is on an embankment, which has concrete sides. You can see on your left the terminus of the Fairbourne Miniature Railway at Penrhyn Point, and Barmouth harbour. Your train will slow to 10 M.P.H. to cross the Barmouth viaduct, which is 800yds long. There is a footpath on the right hand side. Please look at the views up the Mawddach on this side, and contrast its width with that at the harbour side on the left. You pass over a swing bridge and onto the short Borthwen / Orielton Viaducts. The swing bridge and viaducts were used in the filming of the Ghost Train. On the left, in the water, the Barmouth lifeboat is kept. On the right you will see the tollhouse for the footbridge and the Lifeboat Station. You now go through a tunnel of 70yds and cross Old Chapel viaduct before coming to Barmouth station. As you enter the station there is a crossing. Equipment has been installed for the drivers to operate the crossing barriers. The old signal box restricts their view and until it is removed the station staff will operate the barriers.

ABERMO / BARMOUTH
(25½ Miles)

The station is a passing point on the line and the radio token exchange point. There are two platforms. On the side for Machynlleth there is a booking office and waiting room. On the platform there is a toilet for disabled use. There are steps up to the main entrance, but at the north side of the building there is a slope onto the platform. To get to the Pwllheli platform, go across the level crossing and turn right. You will see the nearest toilets in front of you and the entrance to the platform is on the right up a slope. On the inland side from the station is the shopping centre and on the sea side the amusement park. As you stand in the main entrance you face Station Road, in which there are telephones and The Tourist Information Centre (summer only) is in the old Library on the left.

How to Get There
The station is by the A496. Coming from the Dolgellau direction follow the A496 into the one way system, the road runs alongside the railway line. At the level crossing the station entrance is straight ahead. For car parking turn left over the level crossing and there are coach and car parks and the bus terminus.

From Harlech direction turn right into Station Road. The station is in front of you. For parking follow the road round to the level crossing and turn right across it.

After leaving the station the line once more makes its way to the sea and soon becomes the sea wall and you come to Llanaber.

LLANABER
(Church of the river mouth)
(26¾ Miles)

This station was classified as a halt. It is a request stop and is a short section radio token exchange point. The platform is on the inland side of the line. It is 7" too low and has a shelter.

How to Get There

The station is down a rough footpath off the A496, there is no way of turning a car at the bottom of the track.

After Llanaber the train will go over a level crossing and you are in the Snowdonia National Park. The line now moves inland to Tal-y-Bont.

TAL-Y-BONT
(End of the bridge)
(29¾ Miles)

This station was classified as a halt and is now a request stop. The platform is on the inland side of the line and has a shelter. There is a ramp up to the platform.

How to Get There

The station is down a lane from the main road A496. The lane is on the Barmouth side of the bridge in the centre of the village. Approaching the railway the road goes over the line, take the road on the right. There is a turning area here, and the entrance to the platform is under the bridge.

You next come to Dyffryn Ardudwy.

DYFFRYN ARDUDWY
(30¼ Miles)

This is a request stop. The station was an old passing point, but now only the platform on the inland side is used. It is 7" too low and has a shelter. There is level access onto the platform.

How to Get There

From the A496 take one of the roads going towards the sea and Llanenddwyn. You will come to the level crossing. The station platform is on the right and a small car park on the left.

Leaving the station you will see on the left the site of the old goods yard. The post is still standing for the loading gauge. Also on the left is the Llanbedr Airfield.

LLANBEDR
(Church of Saint Peter)
(32½ Miles)

The station used to be called Talwrn Bach Halt and is now a request stop. The platform is on the sea side of the line and has a shelter. There is a slope to the platform from the level crossing.

How to Get There

The station is on the road from the village to Shell Island and the airport. The road leaves the A496 in the village on the south side of the bridge.

On the left is a stretch of water that is used as a harbour for boats. As you cross the Pensarn River bridge you come to Pensarn.

PEN-SARN/PENSARN
(End of the paved way)
(33¼ Miles)

The station used to be called Llanbedr & Pensarn, it is now a request stop. The platform is on the inland side of the line and is 2" too low. There is a telephone box at the station.

How to Get There

The station is alongside the A496.

The line now heads toward the sea and you come to Llandanwg.

LLANDANWG
(34 Miles)

This station was classified as a halt and was an old passing point. It is now a request stop. The platform is on the sea side of the line. It is 3" too low, and has a shelter. A footpath leads down to the station from the railway bridge.

How to Get There

From the A496 between Harlech and Llanfair take the road to Llandanwg. The station is on the left of the railway bridge. There is no parking allowed on this road for 300yds from the railway bridge.

The line now heads northeast. Looking out on the left you will get a view of Tremadog Bay and if it is clear you may see Snowdon. Next you will see the Royal St David's golf course on the left. Harlech College and the theatre are on the right. After passing the college you get your first view of Harlech Castle on top of the cliff. Over the level crossing on the left is one of the radio masts for the radio token system. Drivers of trains going towards Barmouth operate the barriers from the platform.

HARLECH
(Beautiful slate)
(35¾ Miles)

The station is a passing point and a radio token point. There are two platforms with shelters joined by a footbridge. The Tourist Information Centre (summer only) is in High Street. From the station climb up the road from near the level crossing to the High Street, turn right and it is on your right hand side. The Castle overlooks the station. To get there follow the same road up the hill towards the High Street and the entrance is on your left. In summer there is an entrance near the level crossing. There is also the St David's Golf Course. The nearest toilet for gentlemen and ladies is on the main road between the Queens Hotel and the level crossing.

How to Get There

The station is alongside the A496. The small car park entrance is on the north side of the Queens Hotel. From the car park there is a slope up to the platform for Pwllheli. To get to the other side you can cross over the footbridge or there is a foot crossing at the Barmouth end of the platforms. There is also an entrance to the Barmouth platform from the road on that side of the station.

The train now travels over the flat area of Morfa Harlech to Tygwyn.

TYGWYN
(38½ Miles)

This station was classified as a halt and is now a request stop.

There is only a small platform that is 3" too low on the sea side of the line with a shelter. The station has no lighting, so trains do not stop here early morning or evening.

How to Get There
The station in on the A496, near Ynys where the line crosses the road. The platform is on the Harlech side of the level crossing.

You will soon be able to see the buildings of Portmeirion across the Traeth Bach before you come to Talsarnau.

TALSARNAU
(39¼ Miles)
This is a request stop. The platform is on the inland side of the line and is 8" too low. There is only the overhang of the old station house for protection.

How to Get There
From the centre of the village take the road on the sea side by the Ship Aground, it is marked with a station sign. The station is ¼ mile along the road. The small car park is on the left before the level crossing. There is a slope from the car park to the platform.

Carrying on you come to Llandecwyn.

LLANDECWYN
(40½ Miles)
This station was classified as a halt and is now a request stop. There is only a small platform that is 2" too low on the inland side of the line with a shelter. The station has no lighting, so trains do not stop here early morning or evening.

How to Get There
The station is ¼ mile from the A496 on the road to toll bridge for Penrhyndeudraeth and Porthmadog. There is a slope up to the platform from the road.

The train slows to 10 M.P.H. to cross the bridge over the Dwyryd. As you start to cross the bridge you will leave the Snowdonia National Park for the last time. On the right of the bridge a single-track road runs alongside the line. It is controlled by traffic lights, which are operated from the tollhouse at the far end of the bridge. The open land on the right as you leave the bridge was the site of Cooke's explosives works, the road and line now run into Penrhyndeudraeth.

PENRHYNDEUDRAETH
(Headland between two beaches)
(41¼ Miles)

The station was an old passing point on the line. It is now a single platform that is 6" too low, with a shelter.

How to Get There

The station is on the road for Harlech that leads to the toll bridge. There is a small car park with a slope up to the platform.

The line now follows the north bank of the Dwyryd and on a tight right hand curve heads north into Minffordd. The station is partly under the main road and the Ffestiniog railway.

MINFFORDD
(Lip of the Road)
(42½ Miles)

The station is a single platform that is 3" too low on the inland side of the line with a shelter. This is the nearest point between the Cambrian Coast Line and the Ffestiniog Railway station, which is at the top of the sloping path from the station. Portmeirion is about ¾ of a mile, leave the station and turn right onto the main road, towards Porthmadog. Walk along the road until you come to the pedestrian crossing then take first left, then first right and this lane will bring you to the entrance.

How to Get There

The path entrance is between the main road and the Ffestiniog railway line. The entrance is on the Porthmadog side of the Ffestiniog Railway Station, and it is located on the north side of the A487.

The Ffestiniog Railway Minffordd yard is on the left. Painted on the end of the building is MAENOFFEREN SLATE QUARRY CO LTD. The new hostel can be seen behind it. The exchange sidings between the Ffestiniog Railway and the Cambrian Railway opened in 1872. After the yard you will see on the left the end of the last high voltage grid tower. From here there are cables to the other side of Porthmadog. On the right is the quarry at the side of Y Garth. The line now turns northwest, and the train will travel over the Glaslyn Bridge at 10 M.P.H. On the left by the side of the road track you will notice grey boxes, these are associated with the high voltage cables. You can see the football ground on the right and after crossing the road will come to the Welsh Highland Railway on the right. By the shed a footpath crosses the line, this was the route of the old Welsh Highland Line into Porthmadog. The train will stop at the level crossing for the driver to operate the barriers.

PORTHMADOG
(44½ Miles)

The station is a passing point on the line where the radio token is exchanged. There are two platforms with bus type shelters on each platform. Ramps lead down from the platforms to the main road. Part of the station building has been turned into The Station Inn. The nearest toilets are in the High Street. Turn right on leaving the station and the toilets are on the right hand side. Opposite on the left is the Welsh Highland Railway Porthmadog. You have to walk to the other end of the town for the Ffestiniog Railway. Leave the station and turn right into the High Street, to the roundabout then continue through the main shopping centre to the other end of the High Street. In Snowdon Street there is the Snowdon Pottery, Madog Car & Motorcycle Museum, and by the harbour a Maritime Museum. The Tourist Information Centre

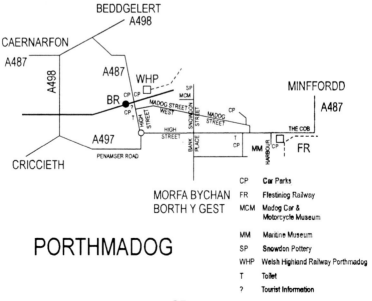

CP	Car Parks
FR	Ffestiniog Railway
MCM	Madog Car & Motorcycle Museum
MM	Maritime Museum
SP	Snowdon Pottery
WHP	Welsh Highland Railway Porthmadog
T	Toilet
?	Tourist Information

37

is in temporary accommodation in the car park next to the railway station.

How to Get There
Take the A487 for Caernarfon from the town centre. The car parks are on the left alongside the station. on the both sides of the level crossing.

The new leisure centre is on the left as you leave the station. The train will cross over the A498 road then run besides the A497 road before crossing over it and heading southwest toward Tremadog Bay. As you come to the shore, on the left, is Graig Ddu/Black Rock. The sands are behind it but you cannot see them from the train. Where the footpath crosses the line was the site of the old Black Rock Halt. As the train enters Criccieth you cross the only gated crossing with semaphore signals that is manned on the line between Machynlleth and Pwllheli.

CRICCIETH
(49½ Miles)
This was a passing point on the line but is now only a single platform on the inland side of the line. The only shelter is under the overhang of the old station building. There is level access to the platform. The station is at the end of the shopping street. You can also visit the Castle.

How to Get There
The station is near the A497. From the centre of the town take the A497 Stryd Fawr/High Street in the Pwllheli direction. Go past the post office and the entrance is on the left between the Station Bakery and Criccieth Gallery Antiques. The road is not named, as it was the old station approach. The old G.W.R. boundary post is still on the left hand side. The station and small car park at the end.

1½ miles after Criccieth you will see on your right the village of Llanystumdwy where Lloyd George lived. You will cross over the Dwyfor and then follow the shore. After crossing the river Wen there is the old junction station of Afon Wen, which still has some of its platforms and buildings standing. The embankment for the Caernarfon line is still in place. The line from here to the holiday camp was doubled in 1947. The line passes through the holiday camp and the station is at the end of the camp.

PEN Y CHAIN
(54 Miles)

This was an old passing point on the line. The station is for the holiday camp. It is now a request stop and the short section for the radio token. The platform has a shelter and a ramp leads up to the lane. At the top of the ramp turn right for the main road.

How to Get There

The lane to the station is off the A497 on the Pwllheli side of the holiday camp.

The line now travels alongside the Morfa Abererch to the station.

ABERERCH
(Mouth of the river Erch, mottled)
(55½ Miles)

This station was classified as a halt and is now a request stop. There is only a small platform on the inland side of the line. The station has no lighting, so trains do not stop here early morning or evening.

How to Get There

From the village take the road in the Criccieth direction to the A497. The lane to the station is nearly opposite. The station is ¼ mile along a lane towards the sea. Part way down the lane it is one way. The station is on the left before the level crossing.

You will see that the area has now mostly a sand base and behind the bank, on your left, is the sea. Entering Pwllheli you first pass the end of the run round loop and then you will see the signal box on the left. This is only used as a ground frame should shunting be required. The end of the line is 57½ miles from Machynlleth.

PWLLHELI
(Pool of salt water)
(57½ Miles)

The station is the end of the line and the radio token will be given up. There is only one platform in use. The station buildings are partly used by a cafe. Also there is a waiting room. For the toilets for gentlemen, ladies and disabled, turn left as you enter the station buildings from the platform. (To get to the front of the building, at the end of the platform turn right and this will bring you to the side of the station. Then turn left for the front of the building, which is in Station Square.) There is a taxi rank outside the front of the station and the bus station is across Station Square. By the roundabout is the Tourist Information Centre. The station is convenient for the shopping centre.

How to Get There

The station is in Station Square, by the roundabout at the junction of Penlan Street, Pen Cob and New Street, that is part of the A497. From the roundabout at the junction go along Pen Cob in the direction of the harbour and turn first left alongside the harbour, here there are car parking spaces. The entrance to the station front is on the left, there is no car parking at the station only room for setting down and picking up passengers.

CHESTER — CHIRK

The first part of the line from Chester and Saltney junction to Ruabon was constructed by the North Wales Mineral Railway and opened in 1846. Shrewsbury Oswestry and Chester Junction Railway built the line from line from Ruabon to Shrewsbury, which opened in 1848. The lines became part of the G.W.R. In 1948 they were in the Western Region of British Railways, and in 1963 became part of the London Midland Region.

To cover the line start your journey in Chester. The train will follow the North Wales Coast line to Saltney Junction where it will bear left onto the single line section to Wrexham. This line is

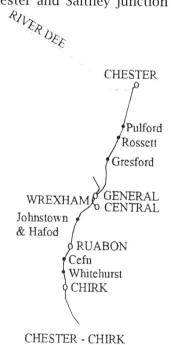

40

the Didcot and Chester Line. The driver will not stop to pick up a token as Track Circuit Block (T.C.B.) protects the line. It is a way of working trains over a track-circuited line with colour light signals. As you pass under the A55 trunk road you will see Balderton on the right. You then go through the short Balderton tunnel of 53yds. After passing under the A483 duel carriageway and going over one more level crossing, you will go over Pulford Brook, and cross into Wrexham County Borough, Wales. The old goods yard of the now closed station at Rossett is on your left. You will see the River Alyn/Afon Alun on your right and then the train starts to climb the Gresford Bank.

The train will cross over the A483. 1 mile further on the right is a cutting for an old railway line that joined the Wrexham Shotton line. The Wrexham Shotton line comes in on your right as you enter the Wrexham. Your line will now become double track. As you enter the station you will see the football ground on the right. The line from Shotton will become single track and then split into two lines. One will go through platform 3 to join up with your line after the station. The other goes into platform 4 and continues to Wrexham Central. Platform 4 and the one beyond, that is not now used, were called Wrexham Exchange.

(Distances on the line are from Chester)

WREXHAM / WRECSAM
GENERAL
(12 Miles)

The station is the main station in Wrexham. It is the junction with the Chester / Shrewsbury line and the Bidston /Wrexham Central line. The station is undergoing a large refurbishment programme and when work is completed there will be full toilet facilities. The Bidston /Wrexham Central trains use platform 4, that has a footpath up to the main road. A footbridge also connects with the platforms of the Chester/ Shrewsbury line, which are 2" too low. There is a lift between platforms 1, 2 & 3, which can be operated by the staff. The booking office is at the entrance to platform 1 from the car park. When leaving the station the shopping centre is to the left, and Wrexham football club to the right. For the Tourist Information Centre turn left into Regent Street, left into King Street, and first right by the Bus Station into Lord Street. Walk to the end and carry straight on down Rhos Ddu Road. The centre is in a light coloured building on your left at the corner of Lambpit Street.

How to Get There

The station is alongside the A451. From the inner ring road take Regent Street (the A451 Mold) and the car park entrance is on the right down Station Approach, which is before you cross the railway line. To get to platform 4, go over the first railway bridge and the footpath is on the right.

As you leave you will notice on the right the Wrexham Brewery and immediately you pass over the line to Wrexham Central. On the right is the old line that formed a triangular junction and went in the Brymbo direction. Shortly you will pass under the Ruabon Road tunnel (64yds), and the Wrexham bypass. Ruabon used to be the junction station for the line to Barmouth Junction and Llangollen.

RUABON / RHIWABON
(17 Miles)

Both platforms have shelters. The access to the platform from Wrexham is on the level but you have to cross a footbridge to get to the platform for Wrexham.

How to Get There

Access is from Station Road, which is off the B5605 just south of the junction with the B5097. There is a small car parking area at the end of Station Road and the gate to the platform is on the right hand side of the old station buildings.

As you leave you will pass under the A539 road to Llangollen, then you cross the line of Offa's Dyke. On your right the old line to Llangollen now disappears under the housing estate. Between here and Chirk the stations of Cefn and Whitehurst are closed. 2 miles from Ruabon you cross the Dee Valley on the Cefn Viaduct (506yds), which is near Newbridge. Looking to your right you will see the Llangollen Aqueduct of the Shropshire Union Canal Llangollen Branch. You go through Whitehurst Tunnel (46yds) under the A5. On the right is Chirk Mariner and on the left a factory with large stacks of wood. Chirk was the terminus of the Glyn Valley Railway. The interchange with the canal was on the right where the industrial estate is now. If you look at the road bridge over the station you can see the opening on the right where the line went under the road.

CHIRK / Y WAUN
(21¼ Miles)

Both platforms have a shelter, and are 2" too low. The only access to the platform to Wrexham is by steps from the footbridge. The platform coming from Wrexham can be accessed from the footbridge or on the level from the car park, which has spaces for 15 cars.

How to Get There

From the centre of Chirk on the B5070 go down Station Avenue. The station is just under ½ mile on the right hand side, after you have passed Cadbury's. Access to the footbridge is on the Chirk side of the line. Next to the station is 'The Poplars', take the road on the Chirk side of this house to get to the car park. The nearest public telephone is just down the lane opposite "The Poplars".

The canal crosses under the road and railway in a tunnel and will appear on your left after you have gone under Chirk Tunnel (51yds). You then cross the River Ceiriog/Afon Ceiriog on Chirk Viaduct (269yds) with the canal below you on the left.

You can also see on the left the old A5 road and the new A5 road viaduct. As you cross over the viaduct you leave Wales.

HAWARDEN BRIDGE — WREXHAM CENTRAL

Several railways constructed the line. The section from Wrexham to Buckley was part of the Wrexham Mold and Connah's Quay railway and was opened in 1866. The extension to Wrexham Central opened in 1887 and the old station at Wrexham was renamed Exchange. In the North the Wirral opened a line to Hawarden Bridge in 1889. The Manchester Sheffield and Lincolnshire Railway had opened a line to Chester Northgate using

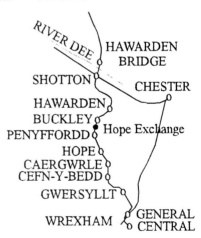

HAWARDEN BRIDGE - WREXHAM

the Cheshire Lines Committee track. They then built a triangle junction outside Chester and came along the north side of the Dee to Hawarden Bridge and across the river to join the line at Buckley. This line was opened in 1890. These lines became part of the Great Central Railway, and then the L.N.E.R.

Your journey begins at Neston. After leaving the station you will eventually go under two bridges and you will see the marsh on your right. Just after the sidings start on the left you cross into Flintshire, Wales. There is a rifle range on the right and a reservoir on the left. You will get a good view of the North Wales coast and the New Bridge across the river Dee at Connah's Quay. You have a high bank on the right before you see Shotton Steel Works. The train will slow down to take the curve, which was part of Dee Marsh Junction. It formed a triangle with the line that went to Chester and Mickle Trafford. On the right you will see the engine shed for the steel works locomotives, before coming to Hawarden Bridge Station.

HAWARDEN BRIDGE

This is a request stop. As the station was built for the use of the steel works only a few trains are scheduled to stop, in the early morning and at teatime. The platforms both have shelters and there is a foot crossing. The approach road and nearby car park belongs to the steel works and is not for public use.

How to Get There

Access is restricted to the footpath alongside the north bank of the river Dee, which is a mile long and comes from the old Queens Ferry Bridge. The path up to the station is near the railway bridge over the river. The other approach is from Shotton, along a footpath over the railway bridge.

As you leave you will cross the river Dee. The first part of the bridge is a swing bridge (287feet long) and was operated hydraulically. The running track can be seen on the right. As you cross you will notice on the left the old Bascule Road Bridge. After crossing the river a line used to come in on the right from Connah's Quay docks. You then cross the North Wales Coast Line and enter Shotton.

SHOTTON

The station has park and ride car park, which have toilets for gentlemen, ladies and disabled. To get to the platform there is a ramp up to the high level. There is a booking office on the side for Bidston. There are shelters on both platforms. To get to the platform for Wrexham you will have to go back to the car park, walk to the main road and cross under the railway line. At the other side of the bridge there is a slope up to the platform from the main road.

To get to the platforms for the coast line you will have to go up to the high level platform for Bidston and walk to the end of the platform. There is a footbridge and steps down to the coast-line. Each of the platforms has a shelter. Alongside the line there is an entrance from the Chester platform, but you will still have to go over a footbridge further along. The platform for Llandudno has a level entrance but the gate is normally locked.

How to Get There

The car park is off the A548 on the Fflint side of the high level line. Turn by the Post Office into Alexandra Street, then first right. The car park is at the end of this street in King Edward Street. N.B. Alexandra Street and King Edward Street are one way streets.

Leaving Shotton the train climbs up to Hawarden station.

HAWARDEN / PENARL G

The station is a request stop. There are shelters on both plat-forms. The small car park has level access to the platform for Wrexham, which is 5" too low. To get to the platform for Bidston, which is 2" too low, you will have to cross by the foot-bridge.

How to Get There

The station approach is on the south side off the B5125. It is on the Chester side of the railway bridge, opposite Trueman's Way. At the bottom there is a small car park.

N.B. There is no access from Station Lane.

As the train leaves you will see the golf course on both sides and you carry on climbing up to Buckley passing under the A55 dual carriage-way.

BUCKLEY/BWCLE

The station is a request stop. The station is at Little Mountain, which is about 1 mile from the centre of Buckley on the A459. The platforms have a foot crossing between them at the Hawarden end, should you have to use it be careful as the line approaches on a sharp bend.

How to Get There

Coming from Buckley on the A459, the lane leading to the small car parking area is on the right before you cross the railway bridge. There is level access from here to the platform for Bidston. On the other side there is a narrow path from Little Mountain to the platform for Wrexham.

On the right as you leave the station is the path of the line that went down to Connah's Quay. You will be able to see the tall chimneys of the cement works at Penyffordd and the works sidings. Look out for the remains of the platforms of Hope Exchange. The line went under your line and ran from Mold junction on the North Wales Coast line to Mold. There was an interchange station here with a branch connected to it from your line. The remains of the track bed can still be seen on the right.

PENYFFORDD

The station is a request stop. There are shelters on both platforms, the platform for Wrexham is 6" too low, and the one for Bidston 6" too low. The car park is on the Wrexham direction side. To get across to the other platform you will have to cross the line on the foot crossing that is at the Wrexham end of the platforms.

How to Get There

The station is near the junction of the A550 and the A5104. From the roundabout take the A5104 (Corwen) road and the entrance to the station car park is on the right.

After leaving you will see a valley on the right in which there is the River Alyn/Afon Alun.

Hope station is a request stop on the Hawarden Bridge — Wrexham Central line.

HOPE/YR HOB

The station is a request stop. Both the platforms have shelters, the side for Wrexham is 9" too low. The only access to this platform is across the foot crossing from the Wrexham end of the other platform. When you get off the train the signs state "Do not cross the line except by crossing". However you may not officially get to this platform as the sign on the other side states "Do not cross the line", so you have no hope of getting a train to Wrexham. Possibly this sign was not replaced when the platform entrance was changed.

How to Get There

There are two ways to get to the station from the A550. Down Sarn Lane for ¼ mile until you pass under the railway bridge, the entrance is on your right. The other way is from A550 in the centre of Hope, a minor road goes towards the A541. After crossing the railway bridge there is a footpath on the left that leads down to the station.

Just before Caergwrle you cross over the river to the other side of the valley.

CAERGWRLE

The station is a request stop. Both platforms have shelters.

How to Get There

The station is alongside the A550. The entrance to the platform for Bidston is on the side of the road. The entrance to the platform for Wrexham is on the Hope side of the railway bridge, from here a slope leads up to the platform.

CEFN Y BEDD
(Ridge of the grave)

The station is a request stop. The entrance to the platforms is from the car park. Both platforms have shelters and are 5" too low. To get to the platform for Wrexham you will have to cross the line by the foot crossing at the Shotton end of the platform.

How to Get There

The car park is alongside the A541. From the junction of the A541 and B5102, which is under the railway bridge, take the A541 in the Caergwrle direction. The entrance is on the right.

Leaving you will cross the road bridge and then the Cefn-y-Bedd viaduct over the River Cegidog that runs into the Alun. As you cross over the river you come into Wrexham County Borough.

GWERSYLLT

The station is a request stop. There are also steps down from Hope Street to both platforms, which have shelters. There is a small car park that is level with the platform for Bidston. To get to the other platform there is a foot crossing at the Bidston end of the platform.

How to Get There

The station is off the A541 in Hope Street. The car park is on the left after leaving the main road.

As you leave, on the left the track bed of the line that went on to the Wrexham Chester line can just be made out. On the right is the site of the triangle junction with the line that went to Brymbo. After passing under the dual carriageway you will see the Wrexham/Chester line on the left. The double track of your line will now join together and split into two single lines, the left-hand one going into platform 3 and joining with the Shrewsbury line. The right hand one will take you into platform 4. This platform and the disused one on the right used to be Wrexham Exchange. The name was changed to General in 1982.

WREXHAM / WRECSAM
GENERAL

The station is the main Wrexham station. It is the junction of the Chester/Shrewsbury line and the Bidston/Wrexham Central line. The station is undergoing a large refurbishment programme and when work is completed there will be full toilet facilities. The Bidston /Wrexham Central trains use platform 4, which has a footpath up to the main road. A footbridge also connects with the platforms of the Chester/Shrewsbury line, which are 2" too low. There is a lift between platforms 1, 2 & 3, which can be operated by the staff. The booking office is at the entrance from the car park, which leads onto platform 1. When leaving the station the shopping centre is to the left, and Wrexham football club to the right. For the Tourist Information Centre turn left into Regent Street, left into King Street, and first right by the Bus Station into Lord Street. Walk to the end and carry straight on down Rhos Ddu Road. The centre is in a light coloured building on your left at the corner of Lambpit Street.

How to Get There

The station is alongside the A451. From the inner ring road take Regent Street the A451 (Mold) and the car park entrance is on the right down Station Approach, which is before you cross the railway line. To get to platform 4 go over the first railway bridge and the footpath is on the right.

The train will now continue down the short branch to Wrexham Central. Passing under the main line you will see on the left the Wrexham Brewery where the lager is brewed.

WREXHAM/WRECSAM
CENTRAL/CANOLFA

The station has only one platform and is at the end of the single line branch from Wrexham General. Trains to and from Bidston use this station. The platform is 2" too low and has a shelter on it. It is alongside a large car park. It is proposed to build a new station a short distance from the present one in the direction of the General Station. The large shopping centre is close by. Leave the station, cross over the road into Priory Street and walk to the end into Hope Street. Part of the shopping area is here. For the Tourist Information Centre go across Hope Street into Argyle Street, walk to the end and turn right into Rhos Ddu Road and the centre is in a light coloured building on your left at the corner of Lambpit Street.

How to Get There
The station is accessed by a footpath alongside the car park at the junction of Vicarage Hill and Priory Street.

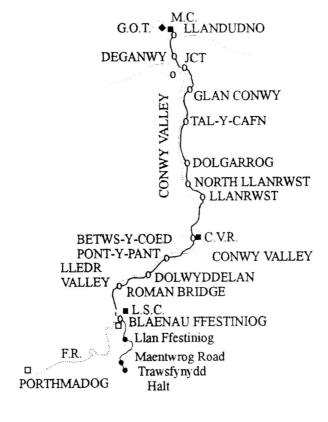

LLANDUDNO - BLAENAU FFESTINIOG

LLANDUDNO — BLAENAU FFESTINIOG

The Chester and Holyhead Railway opened the line from Llandudno Junction to Llandudno in 1858. The L.N.W.R. took over in 1859. The Conway & Llanrwst Railway opened in 1863, and the L.N.W.R. took over the same year. The line opened to Betws y Coed for goods in 1867 and passengers in 1868. The Betws extension opened to Dolwyddelan in 1879 and later in the year through to Blaenau Ffestiniog. The line became part of the L.M.S. and the London Midland Region of British Railways.

LLANDUDNO
(Church of St. Tudno)
(Distances on the line are given from Llandudno)

The station is the end of the line from the Junction. There is a booking office and in the building a waiting room with toilets for gentlemen, ladies and disabled. The access to the platforms is level from the street. Only platforms 1, 2, & 3 are now used. There is a public telephone outside the station and a taxi rank. In Llandudno you can go to the top of the Great Orme on the Great Orme Tramway, and cable cars from Happy Valley. On the Great Orme there are copper mines. The main shopping centre is close to the station, leaving the station carry on straight down Vaughan Street to the roundabout and turn left into Mostyn Street, or carry straight on for the promenade. At 66 Mostyn Street, Mostyn's Cafe has a G gauge tram running round inside. On the left as you go along Mostyn Street is Trinity Square where at 3 & 4 there is the Alice In Wonderland Centre at The Rabbit Hole. Tourist Information Centre is in Chapel Street. To get there from the railway station turn left into Augusta Street, carry on into Madoc Street. At the end of Madoc Street, crossing over Lloyd Street, take the street which is just offset to the right, Chapel Street, the centre is on your left.

How to Get There

The station is at the junction of Vaughan Street and Augusta Street. From the A470 go past the fire station and supermarket. At the roundabout turn left into Vaughan Street. The station is facing you at the end of the road. Improvements are taken place at the station.

Leaving Llandudno the line is soon passing the golf course on the

West Shore of Conwy Bay. Turning left you come to Deganwy. The docks here were built by the L.N.W.R. to take the slate trade away from the Ffestiniog Railway and Porthmadog.

DEGANWY/DGANWY
(1¾ Miles)

The station has two platforms, both are 4" too low. There is a shelter on both platforms and a footbridge connects them. The Junction direction platform has level access from the road. You can get to the Llandudno platform by going over the level crossing and going up the slope to the platform by the signal box. At the crossing end of this platform there are public toilets for gentlemen, ladies and disabled. The station is opposite the small shopping centre.

How to Get There

The station is alongside the A546 Station Road.

Looking across the river Conwy you can see the Castle. The nearest bridge is the newest road bridge, then the old suspension road bridge and finally the tubular bridges of the railway. Entering the Junction the line to Holyhead comes in on the right. The original station was here. The original line up the Conwy valley breached off to the right, near the slip road for the expressway.

For details of Llandudno Junction (3 Miles) see the Chester - Holyhead line.

The driver will collect the token for the line to Llanrwst from the station office. Leaving the junction you pass under a road bridge. The line used to go through the right hand arch, which now leads to the goods yard. You will turn right leaving the main line. Going over a road crossing and under the expressway you will see the Afon Conwy / Conwy River and Conwy over the other side. On the right is a nature reserve. It was here that the original line came in from the junction. The first station is Glan Conwy. It was closed in 1964 and reopened 1970.

GLAN CONWY
(Bank of the Conwy)
(3 Miles)

This is a request stop with one platform, which has a shelter. The platform is 18" too low but a set of steps is provided.

Toilets are by the main road.

How to Get There

The station is alongside the A470. There is a small car parking area and access to the platform is by a slope.

The line now follows the east bank of the river and you enter the Conwy Valley. As the line takes a sweeping right hand bend the A470 road comes in from the left. This is the area where there was a halt for Bodnant Gardens. You may notice some diamond shaped boards on poles either side of the river painted yellow or red, these are where cables go across. Ahead to the right you will see the bridge at Tal y Cafn. When the railway was opened there was only a ferry here. You will soon pass the fixed distant signal for the level crossing. The gates are manually operated and the signalman will show a flag for the train to proceed.

TAL Y CAFN
(8½ Miles)

The station was a passing point and was called Tal y Cafn & Eglwysbach Halt. This is now a request stop with only one platform in use. The platform is 16" too low but steps are provided. There is a gentlemen's toilet on the platform

How to Get There

The station is off the A470. Take the B5279 to Tyn y Groes, and the station is on the right by the level crossing. Before the level crossing on the left is a cafe.

On the left as you leave the station you first pass the livestock market and then the site where a group of railway enthusiasts keep their equipment. The site is not open to the public.

Following the valley you will see on the other bank Dolgarrog, with its hydroelectric power station and aluminium works. A branch was built from the station to the works in 1910 and the bridge can still be used as a footpath. The station was closed 1964 reopened 1965.

DOLGARROG
(11½ Miles)

The station was a halt and is now a request stop. The platform is 7" too low, but a set of steps is provided. There is a ramp up to the platform on which there is a shelter.

How to Get There

The station is on the opposite bank of the river from Dolgarrog. It is 100yds from the A470, down an unmade lane, opposite the entrance to the Plas Maenan Hotel. There is a footbridge over the river, which used to carry the railway line to the aluminium works in Dolgarrog. To get to the village, walk over the bridge and follow the rough path straight on for ¾ mile and you will come out on to the B5106 near the village post office.

The river comes towards the line and then swings away to the other side of the valley where there is Trefriw Wells Spa. Further along you can see the village. Passenger boats used to come here from Conwy. Shortly you will come to Llanrwst signal box on the right. The train will stop while the tokens are exchanged. The signal box operates the semaphore signals but the points are hydro-pneumatically operated and preset for the direction of travel. Past the signal box is the maintenance yard. Here you may see the mechanically operated trolley and trailer used for maintenance work. It is kept on a piece of rail that is higher and at right angles to the running rail. To get the trolley onto the running rail the trolley is pushed onto pieces of portable track, which are laid over the running rails. On the underside of the trolley is a jack, which then lifts it up. The portable track is removed and the trolley swings round on its jack, it can then be lowed onto the running rails. The station was originally called Llanrwst & Trefriw, and then Llanrwst, it is now Llanrwst North.

GOGLEDD LLANRWST NORTH.
(14½ Miles)

The station is now a request stop. It is now the only passing point on the line to Blaenau Ffestiniog. The drivers of the trains will exchange the token here at the signal box. The entrance is onto the Llandudno platform from the car parking area. The platform has a shelter and is 13" too low. To get to the other platform you will need to cross over the line at the Blaenau Ffestiniog end of the platform. Both platforms have a slope down to the crossing. The Blaenau Ffestiniog platform has a shelter and is 10" too low.

How to Get There

The station is off the A470 going from Llanrwst in the direction of

Llandudno. When the road turns over the railway bridge carry straight on and you will come to the station car parking area on your left.

Leaving the station you now enter the single line section to Blaenau Ffestiniog. Going round Llanrwst you enter a cutting and go under an aqueduct carrying a stream down to the river. After Llanrwst tunnel (85yds) you come into Llanrwst. This station was opened when the Eisteddfod was here in 1989. The old station was then renamed Llanrwst North.

LLANRWST
(15 Miles)

It is a single platform with a shelter, and a slope up to the main road. The shopping centre is to the left of the station entrance.

How to Get There

From the centre of the town go along Denbigh Street, the A548 for Abergele. The station entrance is on the right after passing the end of the shops.

The train now makes its way through the town towards the river. When you cross the river you enter the Snowdonia National Park. The line follows the west bank of the river along the valley. You will cross the Afon Llugwy, Swallow Falls is 2 miles upriver from here. As you get to Betws y Coed you will see on the right a set of rails. These are used for the maintenance trolley, so that it can be removed from the line. There are other sets along the line. On the left in the old goods yard is the Railway Museum with its 15" tram and 7¼" gauge railway.

BETWS Y COED
(18½ Miles)

The station was a passing point on the line and classified as a halt. It now has only one platform with a shelter. There is level access to the road. The nearest telephones and toilets for gentlemen, ladies, and disabled, are outside the station. Leave the station, turn left and walk along the road and they are on the right. The Conwy Valley Railway Museum is in the old goods yard across the footbridge. The Motor Museum is by the coach park. Turn right outside the station and walk along the road and you will see it on your left. The Tourist Information Centre is in the Royal Oak Stables. Go out of the station, straight across the road into the park opposite and they are in the building on the right.

47786 on the Royal Scotsman at Betws-y-Coed station, on the Llandudno Junction — Blaenau Ffestiniog line.

Swallow Falls is 2 miles walk up the A5 in the Bangor direction.

How to Get There

There are large coach and car parks by the station.

From the Bangor direction on the A5 continue through the village until you pass the pelican crossing then turn left. From Llandudno follow the A470 until it meets the A5, turn right over the Waterloo Bridge*.

From Blaenau Ffestiniog follow the A470 until it meets the A5, turn left and follow it over the Waterloo Bridge*.

From the south on the A5. This road will lead you over the Waterloo Bridge*.

*After crossing the Waterloo Bridge go past the two petrol stations and take second turn right. The station is on the right and the car parks on the left.

The station was the terminus of the line from 1867 to 1879. There were proposals to build a narrow gauge line from here to Blaenau Ffestiniog following the Conwy valley to Penmachno, up Cwm Penmachno and then through a tunnel from the east. The other idea was to follow the Lledr and tunnel in from the north, this was one that was used. The Betws Extension Railway to Ffestiniog was to be built to the Ffestiniog Railway gauge, or wider, but it was eventually built to the standard gauge.

Before Betws y Coed the curves on the line have not been very tight, but as you leave you immediately start on the tight curves laid on the survey for the narrow gauge line. You soon pass under the A5 road and start to climb. Passing through the Beaverpool tunnel (61yds) you come out onto the side of the valley overlooking the A470. The river Conwy is on the left but it branches into the valley opposite. As you come into Glyn Lledr the river below you is the Afon Lledr. Shortly you go over

Cethin's Bridge, which is a viaduct going over the A470, across the river Lledr and then the valley. From now on the train will stay on this side of the river. On the right you see the black and white buildings of Lledr Hall before entering Pont y Pant lower tunnel (144yds) and coming to the station.

PONT-Y-PANT
(Bridge of the hollow)
(22¾ Miles)

The station was classified as a halt and is now a request stop. The platform is 8" too low and has a shelter.

How to Get There
The station is on a minor road, from the A470 take the lane marked to Plas Hall. After crossing over the river turn right, follow this for ¼ mile and the railway station is on the right.

After the station look on the right over the river to see the road and Youth Hostel. You then go through Pont y Pant upper tunnel (66yds) and up the valley. The river and road are on your right and you will soon see Dolwyddelan.

DOLWYDDELAN
(42¼ Miles)

The station was classified as a halt and was a passing point on the line, it is now a request stop. One side of the old island platform is still used. It is 10" too low and it has a shelter on it. The station is by the car park. To get to the platform there are steps. There is also a rough track from the car park to the end of the platform so you can get up the slope. There are picnic tables at the end of the car park. Dolwyddelan Castle is 1 mile from here, on the A470 in the Blaenau Ffestiniog direction.

How to Get There
At the crossroads in the centre of the village the road leads from the A470 to the station. Follow this road and before you cross the railway bridge the car park is on your left.

As the train swings to the right about ½ mile from the station, look out on the right so you can see Dolwyddelan Castle up on the hill. As the Castle goes out of view you go through Bertheos Tunnel (46yds) and then under the A470. The train swings to the right and you can see Roman Bridge station. On the left is a radio mast.

ROMAN BRIDGE / PONT RUFEINIG
(26 Miles)

The station was classified as a halt and is a request stop. The platform is 7" too low and has a shelter. There is level access from the lane.

How to Get There

The station is ¼ mile along a lane off the A470. There is a telephone at this junction.

As you leave the station notice on the right the set of rails that are for use by the maintenance trolley. You now enter Roman Bridge Tunnel (43yds) and proceed to twist your way up the valley. You get your last view of the river before entering Blaenau Ffestiniog Tunnel on a curve. The tunnel is 3861yds long and the longest standard gauge single bore tunnel in Britain. It will take 3 to 4 minutes to go through the tunnel. The highest point of the line is 790 feet above sea level about ¼ mile from the Blaenau Ffestiniog end. You may hear the engine note on the train change. While you have been in the tunnel you have left the Snowdonia National Park. As you emerge you will see, on the left, the small hydroelectric power station for the quarry, and the original slate wharf for the railway. There is an opening under the road where the slate was brought down from the quarry. This is where the original terminus of 1879 was. The old track bed of the Ffestiniog railway is on the right. On the right is the carriage shed of the F.R. and the old B.R. goods yard on the left. The L.N.W.R. Station of 1881 is on the right with another radio mast. This station closed in 1982 when the new station opened. Going under the road bridge and coming alongside the F.R. track on your right, you will enter the new station, which was officially opened in 1983.

BLAENAU FFESTINIOG
(Heads of Ffestiniog)
(31 Miles)

The station is the end of the passenger line. There is a shelter on the platform. The Ffestiniog Railway uses the platform on your right. Their booking office and shop are by the side of the Queens Hotel. They are agents for railway tickets but are not allowed to supply local ones for the line to Llandudno. The station is in the centre of the shopping area. You can catch a bus in summer from outside the Ffestiniog railway shop to Llechwedd Slate Caverns. The Tourist Information Centre (summer only) is situated on the main road opposite the Queens Hotel. Go to the end of the platform and cross the car park. The centre is in the building across the road.

How to Get There

The station is situated alongside the A470. There are two car parks, one on the same side as the station, by the Queens Hotel. The other is on the opposite side of the main road. The toilets here are in the old Duffws Station of the Ffestiniog railway. There are telephones across the road.

From here the line goes 6¼ miles to Trawsfynydd Halt. It is used for freight only but is up to passenger carrying standard. Proposals have been made for a preservation society to reopen it as a tourist attraction.

The line from Blaenau Ffestiniog to Llan Ffestiniog was originally built to the gauge of 1/-11¾" and opened in 1868 by the Ffestiniog and Blaenau Railway. The G.W.R. opened a line from Bala to Llan Ffestiniog 1882. The F & B was converted to standard gauge in 1883. They laid a third rail so there was uninterrupted traffic during the conversion. The narrow gauge centre rail was then lifted. In 1957 Liverpool Water Works proposed to flood the Tryweryn Valley to created Llyn Celyn. The line closed for passengers in 1960 and freight in1961. The building of the Nuclear Power station at Trawsfynydd required rail connection to take the flasks of spent fuel out. The tracks of the L.N.W.R. & G.W.R. had never been joined as the F.R line had been between them, so an extension was built from the L.N.W.R. station to the old G.W.R. station site in 1964. A railhead was established near the power station entrance at Trawsfynydd Halt. The first flasks left in 1965 and the last on 8th August 1995. However an additional one was required and went on the 29th April 1997.

LLANGOLLEN RAILWAY

The line is on part of the railway that went from Ruabon to Barmouth junction. The Vale of Llangollen railway opened the line from Ruabon to Llangollen in 1861 for freight and 1862 for passengers. It was worked by the G.W.R. The Llangollen & Corwen Railway opened the section to Corwen in 1865. The L.N.W.R. arrived at Corwen the same year from the north. The next section was built by the Corwen & Bala opening to Llandrillo

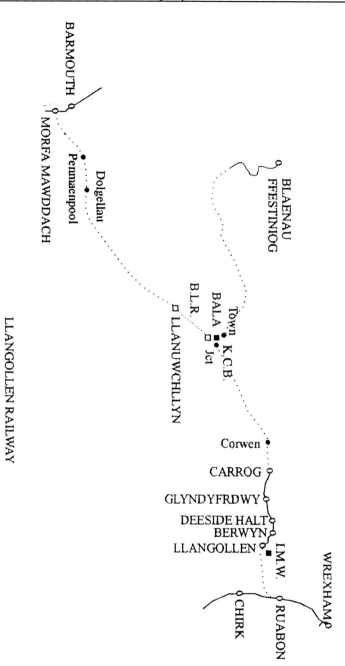

in 1866 and to Bala in 1868. The Bala & Dolgelly (Dolgellau) also opened in 1868. From Barmouth junction, now called Morfa Mawddach, the Cambrian had reached Penmaenpool in 1865 and Dolgellau in 1869. The whole line became part of the G.W.R. and the Western Region of British Railways. The line was closed due to flooding near Bala in December 1964. Services then ran in two sections. The first from Ruabon to Llangollen, and the second from Bala Town to Bala Junction, and on to Barmouth. The whole line was closed down in January 1965. The line had been double track from Ruabon to Llangollen Goods junction west of the station. The rest of the line was single track with passing points. The Flint and Deeside Railway Society reopened Llangollen Station in 1975. The society was renamed in 1977, The Llangollen Railway Society. The society has reopened the line in sections, to Pentrefelin sidings 1981, Berwyn 1985, Deeside 1990, Glyndyfrdwy 1992, and Carrog 1996.

Nearby is Llangollen Wharf from which horse drawn barges take trips along the Canal. Round trips can be arranged by boat and train to Berwyn. The Motor museum also has a display of canal memorabilia. There is the International Model Railway World and the Dr Who exhibitions at Dapol.

LLANGOLLEN
(Distances along the line are given from Llangollen)

The station is the old G.W.R. station. A footbridge connects the two platforms. You will see that the footbridge steps are cantilevered over the river Dee. At the Corwen end of the platform there is a slope up to the bridge from both platforms. Unfortunately there is a 6" step at the top. On the main platform there are toilets for gentlemen and ladies. There is a booking office, shop and cafe. The station is undergoing improvements.

How to Get There
The station is situated on the A539. Coming from Wrexham as you enter the town on the left you will come to Dapol Model Railways (Dr Who Exhibition). Turn into the car park next to it. Walk from there towards the town by the road or river and you will come to the station on your left. From the A5 turn at the traffic lights for Wrexham A539, into Castle Street. Take first left into Market Street and there is a car park and toilets on your left. From the car park return to Castle Street

A Llangollen Railway diesel Class 20 D8142 at Llangollen, an old GWR station closed by British Railways in 1965 and reopened 10 years later.

and turn left, cross the river bridge and the station is on your left. The Tourist Information Centre is in the Town Hall, Castle Street near to the river bridge.

Opening Times & Details
The railway is open most weekends, Easter and daily from May to the end of October.

Detail from: Llangollen Railway, The Station, Abbey Road, Llangollen, Denbighshire. LL20 8SN.

Leaving the station the line is double track to the signal box at the goods yard. Only the line nearest the river is used, the other track is used for storage. The engine shed is on the right as you leave the station but is high up on the bank. The shed line and the main lines meet each other at the Goods junction signal box on the left. Here the token may be exchanged depending how the railway is running. Sometimes off-season when there is only one train in service the line is only split into two sections. From here the line rises at 1:110 to the Berwyn. You will see a track on your right but this only goes into the sidings at Pentrefelin. Here you cross over the river Dee to the opposite bank. The bridge has a speed restriction of 15 M.P.H. Over the other side of the river you can see the canal and you may see the overflow from it coming into the river. On the right you will soon see the suspension bridge crossing the river from the Chain Bridge Hotel. In summer you can take a canal boat from Llangollen to here and return by train or vice versa.

BERWYN
(1½ miles)

The station is a single platform on the left. It is being refurbished therefore the waiting room and toilets may not always be available.

How to Get There

The station is alongside the A5. Steps lead down to the platform. Should you come by canal boat then you can cross the river Dee by the chain bridge and follow the path to the station.

As the train leaves the station you cross the Berwyn viaduct (77yds) on a right hand bend. Look across the river on the right to the horseshoe dam. The water for the canal is taken from here. The gradient now

Llangollen Railway 5MT, 4806 Magpie 2-6-0 at Berwyn station. This class was introduced by the LMS in 1934. The head code indicates it is a stopping passenger train.

increases to 1:80 up the tunnel. On the right you pass the site of the Berwyn loop, which is now only a siding, before you enter the Berwyn/Deeside tunnel (686yds). It is partly on a curve and the gradient in the tunnel is 1:135. Above the tunnel the main A5 road crosses over the top of the line twice. After the tunnel there is a level section of track before you start to climb again. Coming to Deeside halt the points at the Llangollen end are hydro-pneumatically operated point set in the Carrog direction. These pre-set points have a speed restriction on them of 15 M.P.H. There is only a platform on the left side going towards Carrog, and this side of the line is signalled for working both ways.

DEESIDE HALT
(3½ miles)

The halt is a request stop, and is a passing point on the line. There is no road access to the station, but there is a footpath to the river.

The line continues alongside the river and the main road will reappear up on the side of the valley on the left. As you approach Glyndyfrdwy the track goes downhill until just past the station. There are sidings on both sides of the line and the signal box is on the right. The token is exchanged here and the token catcher on the left of the track may be used. Going over the only level crossing between Llangollen and Carrog you enter the station.

GLYNDYFRDWY
(6 miles)

The station is a passing point on the line. A footbridge connects the two platforms. There is a slope up to the platform from the level crossing on the Llangollen side, where there is a booking office, waiting room, and toilets for gentlemen, ladies, and disabled. There is a picnic area at the station. It is possible to get to the Corwen platform up a slope but make prior arrangements.

How to Get There

Turn off the A5 at the post office down the lane to Rhewl. The station is on the left by the level crossing.

As you leave you go over another set of pre-set points, this time in the Llangollen direction. The line continues to rise as it follows the valley. As you start to sweep into Carrog, on a left handed curve, you can

D8142 arrives at Carrog station, at present the terminus of the Llangollen Railway. There are plans to extend the line to Corwen, three miles away.

see the station on the left. The sidings and signal box are on the left. Until the box is used ground frames control the station.

CARROG
(8 miles)

This is the present terminus to the line, until it is extended to Corwen. The station has two platforms. The Corwen side has a shelter and is approached by a sloping path from the road. On the Llangollen side there is a booking office, waiting room, and cafe. The toilet block outside has gentlemen and ladies, both of which can accommodate the disabled. A coach is used in the bay platform as a shop. There is level access from the car park.

How to Get There

From the A5 at Llidiart y Parc take the B5437 to Carrog. The station and car park are on the right after crossing the railway bridge.

It is proposed to extend the line from here to Corwen, 11 miles from Llangollen.

2
NARROW GAUGE LINES

RAILWAY LINES IN NORTH WEST WALES

The question is often asked why are there so many narrow gauge railways in Northwest Wales. The answer can be summed up in two words: slate & mountains.

With the discovery of slate in the mountains quarries were opened up to extract it. Because the quarries were in the mountains the slate had to be transported away from the area for use. Due to the mountainous area to the east it was easier to ship the slate out by sea. Packhorse and boat originally carried the slate down to the wharves for shipment. In some cases the slate was underground so it also had to be mined. The entrances to the mines were very narrow so wagons had to be made small. The wagons in the mines and quarries were laid on tracks. There was no standard to work to so the gauge varied from 23" to 24". With this gauge of track a man could push a single wagon. A narrow gauge could follow the mountain contours with very tight curves. This would not be possible with a standard gauge line.

The first railways, which were worked by horse and rope haulage, were laid to the same gauge as the quarry they were transporting the slate from. This meant that the slate did not have to be transhipped. Every time slate was transhipped there was some breakage.

With the coming of steam more quarries started to build their own lines. In some cases the quarry had its own railway to the sea. In other areas where there are several quarries one railway or several railways would compete to carry the slate. Some of the horse-worked lines were abandoned: others were straightened for steam locomotives.

The first horse worked line was from Port Penrhyn near Bangor to the Penrhyn quarry at Bethesda. It opened in 1801 and was partly re-routed for steam in 1876.

The standard gauge railways were mostly laid around the mountains where the slate was found. They ran along the coast and inland taking an approximate west-east line across North

Wales through Blaenau Ffestiniog. You will notice that the lines to the north became the property of the L.N.W.R and then the L.M.S. To the south they became the property of Cambrian Railways or the G.W.R. and then the G.W.R. To obtain some of the slate traffic the main line railways built branch lines towards the quarries. Two branch line were built to Blaenau Ffestiniog. The L.N.W.R built one from the north from Llandudno Junction. The G.W.R. built one from the south from Bala Junction.

The mountains also contained other minerals besides slate and these were quarried and mined. Many short tramways were constructed to get the slate and minerals to the main narrow gauge and standard gauge lines.

The standard gauge railways brought tourists to the area and narrow gauge lines were opened to cater for them. The Snowdon Mountain Railway was opened in 1896.

The North Wales Narrow Gauge Railway that had opened from Dinas to Rhyd Ddu in 1881 became part of the Welsh Highland Railway. In 1923 a line was constructed from Rhyd Ddu via Beddgelert to Croesor Junction, and on to Porthmadog following the Croesor Tramway.

By the 1930s the demand for slate was decreasing. Roads had been improved and lorries could be loaded at the quarry and the slate transported directly to where it was required so less use was made of the railways. Slowly over the years, some of the narrow gauge lines closed, and in the 1960s standard gauge lines closed down. The preservation movement started in the 1950s and some of the lines have been saved as tourist attractions today.

In 1951 the Snowdonia National Park was formed covering most of North-west Wales. The park goes from the coast in the north to the River Dovey/Afon Dyfi in the south, however most of the working quarries were omitted. If you look on the map you will be able to see this. It is why Llanberis and the quarries in the area, only a few miles from the top of Snowdon, are not in the park. There is also a large area round Blaenau Ffestiniog that is not in the park. So this means that as you travel on the railways in North-west Wales you may not always be within the park.

BALA LAKE RAILWAY
RHEILFFORDD LLYN TEGID

The Bala Lake Railway was built as a tourist attraction on the trackbed of an old G.W.R line. This was part of the standard gauge line from Ruabon to Barmouth Junction, now called Morfa Mawddach. The section from Bala old station to Dolgellau was opened in 1868 and closed in 1965.

The main station for the line is Llanuwchllyn (The village above the Lake). The gauge of the new narrow gauge line is 600mm (1'-11⅞"). The first stock was delivered to the new line in 1971. Services commenced on the first section in 1972, to Llangower. The line was extended to Pant-yr-hen-felin in 1975, and in 1976 the final section to Pont Mwyngyll-y-llyn or Penybont at the Bala end was opened. The total length of the line is now 4½ miles. In 1979 a passing loop was installed at Llangower.

The locomotives normally used on passenger service are coal-fired steam engines. No 3 Holy War was built 1902, and No 5 Maid Marian in 1903. Both these locomotives come from Dinorwic quarry. Maid Marian had been at Bessingham Gardens from 1971 to 1975.

Triassic was built 1911 for a cement company near Rugby, it was taken into preservation eventually coming to the railway in 1993.

There are also diesel locomotives, which may also be used on passenger services. No 11 Meironnydd was built 1973, and No 12 Chilmark was built 1940.

The passenger rolling stock has doors on one side only. All platforms used are on the lakeside of the railway. Most of the coaches are enclosed, but there are a few which have open windows. It is possible to accommodate wheelchair passengers in the guard's van on the train but please check before coming. There are also various types of goods stock that can be seen from the train.

A return trip on the railway will take one hour.

LLANUWCHLLYN
(Church above the lake)

On the station there is a booking office, cafe and shop also gentleman's and ladies toilets. The station has been mostly rebuilt

Bala Lake Railway's No 3 coal-fired steam locomotive Holy War — seen here at Llanuwchllyn — was built in 1902 and originally served at Dinorwic quarry.

in the style of the original station. Parts have been brought here from other sites and have been blended in together.

The signal box is the original one and is connected to the semaphore signals. A display of old railway signalling equipment is being brought together for display in the box.

How to Get There

The village of Llanuwchllyn is situated just off the A494 Bala to Dolgellau road. From Bala drive on the A494 until you pass the end of the lake, shortly you will turn left into the B4403 Llanuwchllyn road.

From Dolgellau turn right into the same road. Follow the B4403 through the village. The entrance to the railway is down a lane on your left, which is signposted for the railway. Should you go under the Railway Bridge you have gone too far. Follow the lane to the end and you will come to the station.

From the large coach and car park there is access to the station for wheelchairs.

Engines arriving will take on their coal and water, before running round the train. Leaving the station the train will proceed towards Bala. You will notice the B4403 on your right side; this road stays close to the railway all the way to Bala. You will soon see Bala Lake on your left.

PENTREPIOD HALT
(1¼ miles. Village of the Magpie)

The first station is Pentrepiod Halt, which has access from the road. This station has been built to replace Flag or Glanllyn, which is only a short distance along the line. Flag 1½ miles is sometimes used for Father Christmas specials, as there is now no access except by rail.

LLANGOWER
(2 miles)

Next you will come to Llangower, where there is a passing loop. The loop is not normally used, as for most of the time the railway only operates one engine in steam. Between the B4403 and Llangower station there is a large car park with a picnic area, including gentleman's, ladies and disabled toilets. It is possible to get to the train by using the gated crossing and the end of the station is ramped.

BRYN HYNOD HALT
(2¾ miles. Hill of the remarkable)

The next station is Bryn Hynod Halt. Here there is a short platform, and room for a few cars to park by the side of the road. The Golf Club Halt is no longer used. As you approach Bala the B4403 crosses over the line.

PENYBONT BALA
(4½ miles. Head of the bridge where a river flows from a lake)

The station at Bala is a short walk from the B4403 on a rough footpath. This path may be difficult for wheelchairs. At the Bala station there is a picnic area and a shelter. Parking is only available on the road. This was the site of the original Bala Station on the G.W.R. line from Ruabon to Dolgelley (Dolgellau). It was closed in 1886 after Bala Junction and Bala Town stations were opened. The G.W.R. reopened a halt here in 1926.

How to Get There

To get to the station at Bala take the B4391 (Llangynog) from the A494 at the east end of Bala. Follow this road until you cross over the River Dee Bridge at the end of the lake. Turn right on to the B4403. The entrance gate to the railway is on the left.

The nearest Tourist Information Centre is at the leisure centre in Bala. It is open every day in summer and Friday to Monday in winter.

Opening Times & Details

The railway is open from Easter to the end of September with a limited service operating out of season. The line is open every day in July and August.

Details from: The Station, Llanuwchllyn, Gwynedd. LL23 7DD.

FFESTINIOG RAILWAY

The history of the railway starts with the building of the Cob. In 1798 W.A.Madocks obtained land to build an embankment. The work took three years and was then partly destroyed by a storm. By 1811 the Cob was constructed across the Traeth Mawr reclaiming about two thousand acres of land. The workers were lodged in barracks at the eastern end of the cob. As W.A.Madocks was the MP for Boston in Lincolnshire the lodgings were called Boston Lodge. This is the present site of the locomotive works.

The construction of the Cob caused the water that had been diverted from the Glaslyn to scour a channel. On this was constructed a harbour called Port Madock, to take large sailing ships. The town is now called Porthmadog.

Before the construction of the Cob slate from the quarries in the Blaenau Ffestiniog area had to be carried by packhorse or cart through Llan Ffestiniog down to Maentwrog. From here it was taken down to wharves on the Dwyryd and put in shallow boats to be taken down river to be transferred to the large sailing ships.

In 1830 Henry Archer and Samuel Holland joined together to promote the railway. An act of Parliament was passed in 1832 but the English spelling was used and the railway was not called Ffestiniog but Festiniog, (which in Welsh is pronounced as Vestiniog.) Today the railway is using Ffestiniog. The line was opened in 1836.

71

The line ran from what is now the area of Blaenau Ffestiniog to Port Madoc via the Cob. The railway was first devised as a gravity railway down hill, the only problem being that there was an incline in the area of the Moelwyn tunnel. The trains had to be winched over the incline. This incline was eliminated with the construction of a tunnel in 1842. The gauge chosen was to be the same as that used in the quarries — 1'-11½". Wagons of this gauge and the size could be manhandled at the harbour without the use of horses. It also meant that the wagons could be loaded in the quarries and taken all the way to Port Madoc without having to be transhipped.

The trains would run down hill by gravity. A brakeman was employed on every fifth wagon, with trains of up to 150 wagons. Horses were used to pull the empty wagons up hill. To return the horses down hill a dandy wagon would be attached to the train in which the horse could travel. The horse would pull the empty wagons up the line until it came to the next crossing point. Here it would be exchanged for the horse in the down train dandy wagon. It would then travel back down the incline in the dandy wagon.

As traffic increased thoughts were given to other forms of motive power. At first steam was not considered an option with such a small gauge. However by 1863 Charles Easton Spooner had the firm of George England & Co. of London build four locomotives. Princess and Mountaineer were delivered in 1863 and Prince and Palmerston in 1864.

In 1842 the railway received permission to run passenger trains from the Board of Trade. In 1867 Welsh Pony and Little Giant joined the fleet of locomotives. To increase the line capacity the railway received an Act to double the line in 1869. The cost of this would have been prohibitive so another solution had to be found. This came in the form of a more powerful locomotive, a double bogie locomotive designed by Robert Fairlie. The first one, Little Wonder, was built in 1870. Further locomotives of this type were added to the fleet: James Spooner (1872), Taliesin (1876 a single bogie version), Merddin Emrys (1879) and Livingston Thompson (1886). In 1979 the railway constructed another double bogie Fairlie in Boston Lodge, Earl of Merioneth.

When the Cambrian coast railway came through to Minffordd in 1867 an exchange siding was built with the railway.

Two standard gauge railways eventually came directly into Blaenau Ffestiniog, the London North Western Railway from Llandudno Junction in the north and the Great Western Railway coming from Bala junction in the south. These railways took some of the slate traffic from the Ffestiniog Railway but at the same time helped to bring in tourists. For more details see Conwy Valley Line.

With the start of the Second World War passenger traffic stopped in September 1939. Throughout the war slate was still carried down to Porthmadog. After the war the increase in traffic which had been hoped for never came. This could be due to several reasons. New materials were being used for roofing, slate was also being sent from the quarries by road. The railway eventually stopped running in August 1946.

In 1951 a group of enthusiasts decided to try and revive the Ffestiniog Railway. Eventually in 1954 the Ffestiniog Railway Trust was formed. The first length of line to be reopened was from Porthmadog harbour station to Boston Lodge across the Cob in 1954. The first motive power was a Simplex engine and Prince. Motive power has slowly been restored, brought from other railways or constructed by the railway.

Slowly as the volunteers cleared the old trackbed and reinstated the track to working order the line extended. Minffordd 1956, Penrhyn 1957, Tan-y-Bwlch 1958, and Dduallt in 1968.

However the way to Blaenau Ffestiniog was blocked from here. The Central Electricity Authority, which became the Central Electrical Generating Board in 1957, had decided to build the Ffestiniog pump storage Power Station scheme at Tan-y-Grisiau. The forming of the lower lake for the scheme caused the Moelwyn tunnel to be plugged on the lakeside. The lower lake when full, flooded the old track bed. The power station was also built over the site of the old track bed. To overcome this problem several routes were surveyed. The final one chosen was to form a spiral at Dduallt to gain height and build a new and shorter Moelwyn Tunnel. The new line would go behind the power station to join the old track bed at Tan-y-Grisiau Station.

The line opened to Llyn Ystradau in 1977 and through to Tan-y-Grisiau in 1978.

This left only 1 mile of track to be completed to get the railway into Blaenau Ffestiniog. In 1977 Gwynedd County Council had decided on a new road scheme which would allow the Ffestiniog Railway to get to the centre of Blaenau Ffestiniog. A new station was built on the site of the old G.W.R. station site, which would accommodate both British Rail and The Ffestiniog Railway. This station was in use by 1982 and officially opened in 1983.

Today the railway operates both diesel and steam locomotives. All the steam locomotives that are owned by the Ffestiniog Railway are oil fired. They include — Prince 0-4-0STT built in 1863/4.

Merddin Emrys 0-4-4-0T built in1879.

Earl of Merioneth/Iarll Meirionnydd 0-4-4-0T built in1979.

David Lloyd George 0-4-4-0T built in 1992.

Mountaineer 2-6-2T built in 1917 by the American Loco Co.

Linda and Blanch both 2-4-0STT, built in 1893 are ex Penrhyn Quarry, both have had a front truck and tender added after coming to the Ffestiniog.

The locomotives usually travel with the boiler facing Blaenau Ffestiniog, the exception being Fairlie locomotives which have a boiler at each end.

There are also a number of diesel locomotives used on both passenger and works trains. Two of them may be seen on passenger trains. Both are 4wDM, Castell Conwy/Conway Castle built in 1958 and Upnor Castle built in 1954.

With such a large fleet some of the locomotives will be out of service for maintenance, and some may even be in use on the new line at Caernarfon.

The railway has also purchased some large diesel locomotives built in South Africa by Funkey. These are being adapted to the Ffestiniog loading gauge. They then will be used for passenger trains both on the Ffestiniog and the Welsh Highland Line at Caernarfon.

There are also some privately owned locomotives, which may be seen on the line. Britomart 1899, 0-4-0ST, Palmerston 0-4-0 STT, Monarch 1953 0-4-4-0T are coal fired. If the weather is dry there is a restriction placed on travelling through the forest as they present a fire risk. It is hoped to convert Monarch to oil firing so that it can be used on the whole line.

Some of the old locomotives can still be seen. Welsh Pony 1867 is on a plinth outside Harbour station and Prince 1863 is in the museum there. Livingston Thompson 1886 and K1 that came from Tasmania are both on long term loan to The National Railway Museum at York.

The railway was the first to use bogie coaches in 1871. The coaches used on the line today can vary from very old stock, which is used on vintage trains, to open corridor stock on which light refreshments are served. The modern set is also heated for winter. This set can be used as a push pull set with a diesel engine at the Blaenau Ffestiniog end, the driver controlling the train from the front coach on the trip down to Porthmadog. Most trains carry an observation coach at the Porthmadog end for which there is a supplementary charge. Some of the coaches have wide doors to take wheelchairs. Wheelchair passengers should check with the railway to see if the train you intend catching has one of these coaches.

The new coaches have inward opening doors. The old stock with outward opening doors will have the doors locked by the guard before the train leaves the station. Remember this is not a standard gauge railway so **do not lean out of the windows** as in places there is **zero clearance**. When the line started to carry passengers the maximum width possible was used in making the coaches, therefore there are very tight clearances on the line.

The railway also owns a large variety of goods stock, some of which can be seen on open days at Minffordd yard

PORTHMADOG HARBOUR STATION

The station has a booking office, shop and cafe with a small museum. The cafe serves both hot and cold meals, there is also a small bar. The station is on the level and is accessible to wheelchairs. Toilets at the west end of the station platform include ladies, gentlemen's and disabled. The disabled also have nappy changing facilities. Should you find the toilet locked please ask in the shop or the guard for a key.

How to Get There

The station is situated alongside the A487 at the south end of the High Street.

From the Cambrian Coast line British Rail station, at the level crossing turn right into the High Street follow the street to the roundabout and continue down the High Street. The station is at the far end on the right-hand side after crossing over the Britannia Bridge.

There is a car park outside the station, but this is not very big. Should this car park be full there are two car parks available, for the nearest return to the High Street (A487) turn left. Cross the Britannia Bridge then turn first left, there is a small car park on the right. In the summer season this is used on Fridays for a market.

The main car park, return to the High Street (A487) turn left, cross the Britannia Bridge then first right by the petrol station. Follow this road round the corner, take first right and the car park is in front of you.

The platform is low and to board the train you are required to step up. Some of the coaches have been adapted to take wheel chairs. Try to get a seat on the far side of the coach from the platform. This will give you the best views after Penrhyndeudraeth as you travel up the line. Due to the very tight clearances on the line the old stock with outward opening doors will be locked by the guard before you leave. Should you be in one of these coaches and need to get off the train at a station before Blaenau Ffestiniog let the guard know.

The signals at the station are hand operated semaphore. On leaving the station you can see on the right the signal for trains approaching the station, this a somersault type is not very common. As the train crosses the Cob on the right in the direction of travel is the sea and on the left Afon Glaslyn. To stop the sea from entering the Afon Glaslyn gates are fitted to the bridge, which crosses the Afon Glaslyn behind the Tax offices. When the sea is higher than the Glaslyn the gates close with the weight of water. When the Glaslyn is higher than the sea the gates open. As the train takes the sharp left curve at the end of the Cob you can see Boston Lodge Works on the right. Public are not allowed into the works except on special open days.

(N.B. The distance and height shown are from Porthmadog Harbour Station.)

BOSTON LODGE
(1 mile/25 feet)

This is a request stop, there is no accommodation for waiting for the train.

After the train has left Boston Lodge you will notice on the left-hand side the main road climbs until it is level with the railway. There is a layby here; this was the crossing point of the railway while the new main road bridge was built. You will now notice the old road continues on the right. The guard will put on the carriage lights before the train passes under the bridge, which seems like a small tunnel, this is due to the road crossing the railway at an angle.

As the train proceeds you will notice a large limestone quarry on the left side. Further on the train passes over an ungated level crossing. After this on the left you will see Minffordd yard. This is used by the permanent way department and also has the Hostel for the volunteers. Public are not allowed into the yard except on special open days. The track from here to the Minffordd station appears to be double but is in fact two single lines, one for Boston Lodge and one to Minffordd yard.

How to Get There

The access is from the A487 by a slope from the road on the Minffordd side of the tollhouse. There is no car park but you can park in a small layby on the main road.

MINFFORDD

(2 miles/85 feet)
(Lip of the Road)

The station is a crossing point on the railway. The trains cross on the right hand side on the Ffestiniog Railway. The token may be exchanged here when the station is open. There is a small waiting area under cover. The signals are electric colour lights.

This is the station to alight if you wish to visit Portmeirion, which is about ¾ of a mile. Leave the station, turn right on to the main road towards Porthmadog. Walk along the road until you come to the pedestrian crossing then take first left, up the lane then first right and this lane will bring you to the entrance.

How to Get There

The station is on the A487 on the left-hand side coming from the Porthmadog direction. The small car park is on the Penrhyn side of the station. There are interchange facilities with the Cambrian Coast line, which crosses under the railway just before the station.

Should you come by this train walk up the slope and the Ffestiniog station is in front of you. The slope is at the Porthmadog end of the platform.

PENRHYN
(Headland between two beaches)
(3 miles/160feet)

The name of the village is Penrhyndeudraeth. There is a canopy over the station. The station is used as a hostel and only has room for a few cars. After the train leaves the station it will go through a level crossing over the A4085. Shortly after this you enter the Snowdonia National Park.

How to Get There

The station is on the A4085. From the centre of Penrhyn take the A4085 towards Llanfrothen. The station is on the left. Access to the station is by a sloping path or by a narrow road. The main car park and toilets are at the bottom of the hill in the High Street.

RHIW GOCH
(Red Bank)
(4¼ miles/225feet.)

This is a passing point on the railway and there is no station here. The lines are both signalled for two way working with electric colour lights.

The passing loop is usually only used on special occasions and trains normally use the left-hand line in the up direction. When coal fired steam locomotives are used they usually terminate here due to the fire risk in the forest.

PLAS HALT
(6¼ miles/375 feet)

This small request halt situated on the left-hand side of the track has a shelter. The halt has only footpath access from Plas Tan-y Bwlch, Snowdonia National Park Study Centre.

TAN-Y-BWLCH
(Under the pass)
(7½ miles/430 feet)

This is the main crossing point of the railway. There is a cafe, shop also ladies, gentlemen's and disabled toilets. Should you find the toilet locked please ask in the shop or the guard for a key. The access to the island platform is by a footbridge. Wheel chair and disabled passengers may cross by a level crossing. A locked gate controls this. The key can be obtained from the Cafe or the guard of the train.

Up steam trains may take on water at this station. At the station the single line token will be exchanged. The signals are electric colour lights. From here to Blaenau Ffestiniog the line has no passing points. This restricts the number of trains that can be run beyond here to Blaenau Ffestiniog. After the train leaves the station it crosses Creua Embankment, which is made of stone, and there are fine views of the area. Keep your head inside the coach as in ½ mile you will go through Garnedd Tunnel that is 60 yds long and has very tight clearances

How to Get There

To get to the station turn off the A487 at the Oakley Arms on to the B4410. Follow this road past Llyn Mair until you see the railway bridge. The entrance is a sharp right turn just before the bridge. There is a large car park. There are various walks from the station.

CAMPBELL'S PLATFORM
(9 miles/510 feet)

This is a small hut on the right hand side of the line, it was built to serve the local house before there was any road access.

DDUALLT
(Black Hill)
(9½ miles/540feet)

This was the terminus of the line for many years while the diversion was constructed. The passing loop has now been removed and the arms removed from the signals. It is a request stop and has a shelter. There is no road access to the station. You can however walk there by footpath. With good walking boots on a nice day you can walk the 2 miles to Tanygrisiau following part of the old track bed.

As the train leaves Dduallt it enters a spiral, and climbs up a steep incline crossing over the line from Porthmadog. After completing a full circle it runs parallel to the old track bed which can be seen on the right hand side. On what appears the top of a hill on your right you can see the closed Trawsfynydd Nuclear Power

Station. This is in fact at the north end of Trawsfynydd Lake. As the train proceeds the entrance to the old tunnel is on the right. This was opened in 1842 and was 730yds long. The 1836 to1842 original track used to climb over the hill. The train enters the new tunnel that is only 294yds long. On leaving the tunnel on the right you can see Tanygrisiau Lake. Should the lake be at low level then the old track bed can be seen again.

As the train crosses behind the Power Station the line is on a bridge which was constructed over the pipes, which carry the water needed for the pump storage power station. It is hard to tell where the bridge is situated because of the landscaping. The train then passes over two level crossings, between the two crossings you leave the Snowdonia National Park. The Ffestiniog Pumped Storage Power Station Visitor Centre is on your right with a cafe alongside. Also notice the waterfall on the left-hand side just before the train enters Tanygrisiau station.

TANYGRISIAU
(Under the Steps)
(12 miles/640 feet)

The Station is a single platform on a curve. This will become an island platform when work is completed on a passing loop. A short siding has also been constructed here. There is a waiting room and a car park. The signal box has been constructed and semaphore signals will be installed. These are being operated by electric motors.

How to Get There

The entrance to the station is on the A496. As you leave the A496 the road forks, take the left-hand road and follow the signs for the Power Station. Go past the first car park on the right hand side of the road. You will then come to the Station and car park on the right. The Visitor Centre and cafe are just along the road.As the train leaves Tanygrisiau you will see the village on the right hand side. Further on you will see the Ffestiniog railway site on the left at Glanypwll (near the pool). The original track carried straight on towards the first terminal station at Dinas and the quarries. From here to Blaenau Ffestiniog station the track is wide enough to take two lines. The line now crosses the road once more by a level crossing. You now pass the site of the

old Ffestiniog station on your left, across the road you will see
the old L.N.W.R. station. The train goes under the A496 and
under another road bridge. The other line is now on your left
until you enter Blaenau Ffestiniog station.

BLAENAU FFESTINIOG
(Heads of Ffestiniog)

The Ffestiniog Railway 0-4-4-0T David Lloyd George passing
Tanygrisiau on the approach to Glanypwll.

You have now come to the end of the line having travelled 13½
miles and climbed 710 ft. The word Ffestiniog is a fortification
From the train the platform is normally on the left with the
run round loop on the right. The platform is an island platform
and special trains may use the side nearest the standard gauge
line. There is a canopy over part of the station. On the platform
are ladies gentlemen's and disabled toilets. Should you find the
toilet locked please ask in the shop or the guard for a key. From
the platform a ramp leads up to the bridge. Cross over the
bridge and turn left down the slope for the Conwy Valley Line.
The Ffestiniog Railway shop and booking office is in the base-

ment of the Queens Hotel. Buses for Llechwedd Quarry also leave from outside the shop. To get there cross over the bridge turn right down the steps and across the car park. You can also walk to the main road and turn right. Walk down the road past the bank and turn right at the car park entrance. The shop is on your left. It is hoped to construct a crossing over the Conwy Valley line to the car park from the end of the Ffestiniog plat-form. The Tourist Information Centre is in the building across the road from the Queens Hotel.

Should you be catching the train from here try to get a seat on the far side of the coach from the standard gauge platform. (Left hand side in the direction of travel). This will give you the best views as you travel down the line.

How to Get There
The station is situated alongside the A470. There are two car parks, one on the same side as the station by the Queens Hotel. The other is on the opposite side of the main road. The toilets here are in the old Duffws Station of the Ffestiniog railway. There are telephones across the road.

Opening Times & Details
The journey from Porthmadog to Blaenau Ffestiniog takes between 60 and 70 minutes. The turn round at Blaenau Ffestiniog can be 10 to 15 minutes. Sometimes this can be longer when the train is timed to make connections with the Conwy Valley Line trains. Allow at least 2¾ hours for your round trip.

There are booking offices at Porthmadog and Blaenau Ffestiniog. Through booking is available from some of the standard gauge pay trains and station, this can be cheaper than booking to the nearest Ffestiniog station and rebooking on the railway.

The railway normally operates a weekend service from mid February to Easter then daily to the end of October. Weekend services in November, with Santa Specials in December and daily between Christmas and New Year.

Details from: Ffestiniog Railway, Harbour Station, Porthmadog. Gwynedd. LL49 9NF.

LLANBERIS LAKE RAILWAY
RHEILFFORDD LLYN PADARN

The Llanberis Lake Railway operates on the north shore of Llyn Padarn in an area now known as Parc Padarn. Even though this area is so near Snowdon it is not in the Snowdonia National Park as most of the village and the two lakes are not in the park.

The quarry built the port of Port Dinorwic at Y Felinheli so that the slate could be loaded onto ships. The port is on the Menai Strait between Bangor and Caernarfon. The slate was carried by boat down Llyn Padarn and then carried over land to Port Dinorwic. In 1824 the first line from the Dinorwic quarry ran from higher up the mountain and was horse and gravity worked with a gauge of 1'-10¾". (You will notice two spellings Dinorwic the name of the village and the one used by the power station Dinorwig.)

With the coming of steam a more level route was required for the Railway, and a new line was built along the lakeside and on to Port Dinorwic in 1843. The gauge was 4'-0", the line being known as the Padarn Railway. The slate was brought down from

Outside the engine shed which is part of the Welsh Slate Museum complex stands Thomas Bach — Little Thomas — on the Llanberis Lake Railway still looking spruce although built in 1904.

the upper quarries to the railway in 2 feet gauge wagons. The wagons on the 4'-0" line could take four of the 2 feet gauge wagons. The line operated trains for goods and the quarry workman. The line was closed in 1961 and the track lifted. The quarry finally closed in 1969.

One of the original locomotives, Fire Queen, can be seen at Penrhyn Castle Museum at Llandegai Bangor. This is on the A5122 about 2 miles from Bangor going towards the A55 and Conwy.

Though the first railways were constructed mainly for the removal of slate from the area the Llanberis Lake Railway was built as a tourist attraction. The present railway uses part of the lakeside route of the old Padarn Railway. Construction started in 1970, part of the line opening in 1970 and all the way to Penllyn in 1972. The gauge of the line is 1'-11¾".

It is normally worked by coal fired steam locomotives: -

No 1 Elidir built in1889 and painted maroon.

No 2 Thomas Bach (Little Thomas) built in1904 and painted blue.

Both came from Dinorwic Quarry.

No 3 Dolbadarn and painted yellow built 1922 for use in Port Dinorwic Harbour being brought to Dinorwic Quarry in 1936.

The locomotives usually face in the Penllyn direction, but there is a small turntable outside the sheds on which they can be turned.

The diesel locomotive No 8 Twll Coed built in 1952 worked at various locations before being obtained for the railway in 1976. It can be used on passenger traffic. There are also other diesel locomotives, which are used on maintenance work.

The coaches have all the doors on one side and one set of coaches has a specially adapted coach to take wheelchairs. Wheelchairs can also be carried in the guard's van of the trains if there is room.

GILFACH DDU
(Black retreat)

The station at the Llanberis end, Gilfach Ddu, has a booking office, cafeteria and shop. You will notice the goods stock on the siding nearest the car park. After the incoming train arrives the locomotive will be uncoupled and move forward. It will then take

A centenarian still going strong — Llanberis Lake Railway's No 1 locomotive Elidir, built in 1889, at Gilfach Ddu station.

on coal and water as required before running round the train. As the train leaves the station look out for the carriage sheds on the left. Soon you will pass under a bridge and the lake will be on your left. The train on the outward journey will carry on to Penllyn at the far end of the line, a distance of 2 miles. This will take about 15 minutes.

You may notice as you travel along some grey boxes that are about 4' tall and 2' wide by the side of the railway. These are used in connection with the 400kV cables, which run along under the track. The cables are the connections from Dinorwig Pump Storage Power Station to the National Grid Substation at Pentir, which is south of Bangor. You will notice on your right after passing Cei Llydan a stone building with a line running into it. This is for pumping the cooling water into the trench that carries the cables, the water returning to the lake.

CEI LLYDAN
(Wide Quay)

When there are two trains running you will pass the other train at Cei Llydan which is the halfway point. On reaching Penllyn (Head of the lake) the engine will run round the train and proceed back to Cei Llydan. Here it will wait for a few minutes. If you have time you can cross the line and stop at the picnic area by the side of the lake. Tables and seats are provided. You can catch a later train back.

Should you have the time it is well worth a visit to Cwm Derwen woodland and wildlife centre that is next to the station. Here there is a visitor centre and shop. For a small extra charge you can also walk in the woodlands, which include Welsh oak trees. This walk is unsuitable for wheelchairs or pushchairs and strong footwear is recommended. There is an adventure playground for the children.

When the other train arrives, the drivers will exchange the section token and your train will complete its journey back to the main station. You will notice that the tracks continue past the station and across the road to the car park into the side building of the Slate Museum. This is used as the locomotive shed and the workshops for the railway. Should you arrive very early or still be there when the railway closes, you may be treated to the sight of one of the locomotives crossing the road.

How to Get There

Should you come by bus in the season it will take you to the car park by the station. Out of season the bus will drop you on the main road near the visitor centre for Dinorwig Power Station, Electric Mountain. To walk to the railway follow the instruction below.

Llanberis is on the A4086 entering Llanberis from the east, the Capel Curig side, go past the Snowdon Mountain Railway and take the first road right to Parc Padarn*. Arriving from the west Caernarfon side, follow the A4086, which by passes the village, and continue until you go past the village car park and visitor centre for Dinorwig Power Station, Electric Mountain. Take first left to Parc Padarn*.

*Carry on down the road till you cross over the area between the two lakes, Llyn Padarn on your left and Llyn Peris on your right that is used as the bottom lake for the Dinorwig Power Station. Take the next turn left for Parc Padarn and go past the side of the Slate Museum. You will see the station in front of you. Turn left into the coach and car park, where there are toilets for gentlemen, ladies, and disabled, a telephone, and Welsh craft shops.

The slate museum is also here. It is open every day in summer and Monday to Friday in winter. There are old quarry railway items and a display showing the history of slate in the area. It is well worth a visit if you are interested in the history of the area. There is a cafeteria and children's play area. Nearby is the old miner's hospital, in which there is a snack bar. There are also lots of walks through the parc. Other attractions in Llanberis are the village with its shops. The Snowdon Mountain Railway is covered in a separate article. Electric Mountain has displays on the generation of electricity and on Dinorwig Pumped Storage Power Station in particular. Trips can be arranged to visit the power station. The centre has a cafeteria and a large coach and car park. The Tourist Information Centre is open every day in summer and Wednesday to Sunday in winter. It is situated in High Street on the left hand side walking from the railway. It is on the corner of Stryd Goodman/Goodman Street. The High Street is the main shopping street and is the road that joins the by-pass opposite the Electric Mountain visitor centre.

Opening Times & Details
The round trip without a break will take about 40 minutes.

The Railway usually opens for Easter until the end of October. There is a limited service during early and late season. It is open every day in July and August.

Details from: Llanberis Lake Railway, Llanberis, Caernarfon, Gwynedd. LL55 4YT.

SNOWDON MOUNTAIN RAILWAY LLANBERIS
This railway was built as a tourist attraction from the start. Its main purpose was to get visitors from Llanberis to the top of Snowdon/Yr Wyddfa. The line was first opened in 1896. The railway is worked by a rack-and-pinion Abt system, which had been developed in Switzerland. In the centre of the tracks there is a double rack rail. On the locomotive axles there is a central pinion that engages with the rack, and can be used for driving or breaking. The wheels are free to turn on the axles. The gauge of the track is 800mm (2'-7½").

The distance from Llanberis Station to the Summit is just over 4½ miles. The journey up will take 1 hour, your train will then wait for ½ hour. The return will also take 1 hour, therefore the round trip takes 2½ hours.

Some of the locomotives are the original coal fired steam engines. There are 5 steam locomotives available, supplemented by 4 diesel locomotives. The railway also has 3 diesel electric railcars which can be used singly or in 2 or 3 car multiples. They are not normally used as a single unit.

The steam coal fired locomotives are all 0-4-2T built at the Swiss locomotive works in Winterthur.

No 2 Enid built 1895.

No 3 Wyddfa built 1895.

No 4 Snowdon built 1896.

No 5 Moel Siabod built 1896.

No 6 Padarn built 1922. named Sir Harmood until 1928

No 7 Ralph built 1923.

No 8 Eryri built 1923.

No 7 & No 8 are both stored at Llanberis without boilers.

No 7 was originally named Aylwin then renamed Ralph Sadler which was shortened to Ralph in 1989.

You will notice that the boilers slope down towards the front, this is so they will be level when climbing up the mountain. The shed can be seen from the end of the Llanberis platform.

Hunslet Engine Co., Leeds, built the diesel locomotives.

No 9   Ninian built 1986

No 10 Yeti built in 1986.

No 11 Peris built 1991

No 12 George built 1992.

The diesel electric railcars were built in 1995 by HPE Tredegar Ltd, Tredegar, and carry the numbers 21, 22 & 23.

Lancaster Carriage & Wagon Co. Ltd built the original coaches in 1895. They carry the numbers 2, 3, 4, 5, 8. They also built a flat truck. A Caboose car with a 700 gallon water tank has been built on one of the original carriage frames. In 1923 coaches 6 & 7 were built by Schweizerische Industrie-Gessellschaft, Neuhausen.

All the coaches carry 59 passengers and the guard. The coaches were built with the top section open to the weather but they are now fully glazed. In 1987 East Lancashire Coachbuilders Ltd built coach 10 that can carry 53 passengers and the guard.

LLANBERIS
(341ft/104m above sea level)

The station at Llanberis has a booking office, cafeteria and gift shop. In the adjoining building there are toilets and a small shop selling snacks. The station has two platforms, one is used for arrivals and the other on the booking office side for departures. At the present time each train consists of only one coach and locomotive. With the line being single with passing loops the number of trains is restricted to the time trains can cover the distance between the loops. This gives a ½ hour service. Each platform is long enough to accommodate two trains. This allows two trains with a time gap between to operate behind each other at peak times and increase the number of passengers that can be carried. The railway is now controlled by radio from a control room near the end of the up platform.

The entire railway is built on a slope. The locomotive is always at the lower end of the coach. The front of the locomotive faces the coach in the upward direction. One of the unique things about the railway is that the coaches are not fastened to the locomotive. You will notice that there are only some safety chains and communicating cables between the coach and loco- motive. The present day coaches are fully enclosed for your pro- tection from the winds on the mountain.

Before the train leaves you will notice that the guard is seated at the front of the coach at the controls. He will give signals to the driver for starting and stopping. As the train leaves you will pass the engine sheds on the right and the carriage sheds on the left. The line now rises and will shortly pass over the Afon Hwch. This lower viaduct has fourteen arches, each arch is 4ft higher then the previous one. You will then pass onto the upper viaduct, which has four arches. This gives good views of part of the village. Should you have time it is worth walking to this viaduct and watching a train cross over from the road. It may be hard to believe being so near Snowdon but the station at Llanberis is not in the National Park. As the train crosses the viaducts you will cross a road. This is the point where the boundary for the park comes in from the east, your left. It then follows the railway line up until just before Waterfall station and at this point turns west.

After leaving the viaduct you will soon get your first view of

Snowdon summit and pass the old station of Waterfall ½ mile 600 ft/183m. (The distances given at the stations are from Llanberis and the height is above sea level.)

HEBRON
(1 mile 1069ft/326m)

The train will continue until it reaches the first passing point Hebron. You will notice on the passing points the up line is straight and the loop is to your right. This was done so that if the line were to be double tracked the up line would not have to be moved.

The station points are now controlled automatically by the train. The power for operating the signal lights and the electrical operated hydraulic pump, is supplied by batteries, which are charged up by small wind generators, which you can see by the station. The points are worked by hydraulic ram. The points are normally set for the right hand line. As your train arrives the locomotive operates a trip. This then switches on the signals, the points are set for the left-hand track, and the lights will give the driver the indication to proceed into the station. As the train enters the station it will operate another trip to reset the point.

The train driver will now inform control that the train has arrived. He will now have to wait for permission to proceed on to the next section. Unless you are on an early morning train you will have to wait for the down train or trains to get into the loop. The signals are not used for permission to proceed but are only an indication of the state of the points. Should you have a long wait you will notice that the signal lights go out. This is because they are on a time controller to save electricity.

When your driver has been given permission to proceed the train will move forward. This will operate another trip and the signal lights will come on. As the points are normally already set for your train you will be able to proceed without stopping. As the train climbs up keep looking back at the views. You will be able to see Llyn Padarn. Also on your left you will see parts of Llyn Peris and the road below, where the cars look like toys.

HALFWAY
(2¼ miles 1641ft/500m)

The train will climb up the line to Halfway the next station. The

The grandeur of Snowdonia is captured in this view of the Snowdon Mountain Railway's No 5 Moel Siabod approaching Clogwyn.

crossing point is also controlled here automatically. The same procedure will be carried out here as at Heron. In very bad weather trains may terminate here. As the train climbs up you will see the water of Llyn Du'r Arddu on your right.

CLOGWYN
(3½ miles 2556ft/779m)
The next stop is Clogwyn Station. This station is manned and the points are changed manually. In the early and late season this may be as far as the railway runs. This is for safety as high winds and ice may prevail on the summit, even if at Clogwyn there may be sunshine and very pleasant conditions. As the train proceeds up notice the drop on each side of the line. On your left you will see the waters of the Glaslyn and further away Llyn Llydaw.

SUMMIT
(45⅝ miles 3493ft/1065m)
The Summit Station is the highest point on any railway in Great

91

The Snowdon Mountain Railway's No 10 Yeti at Clogwyn.

Britain. Here there are two platforms, one will usually be occupied with the previous train. Your train has climbed 3152 feet in 45⅜ miles, actual distance 8228yds giving an average climb of 1:7.8. The train will wait here for ½ hour before descending. At the summit there is a cafe and toilets. There is no water or electricity supply to the buildings, the electricity is generated by diesel powered combined heat and power units. There is no road access to the summit and the railway has to bring up all the water and fuel. The summit of Snowdon is 3560ft/1085m and it is only a short walk up from the station. At peak periods each train will be coming up full, a return seat is only guaranteed on the train you came up on. You will only be allowed to travel on a later train if there are spare seats. This also applies should you want to catch a train at one of the intermediate stations.

As the train returns the coach will not need to be pulled but it will roll down under its own weight. The locomotive will use its braking power to hold the coach.

How to Get There

Llanberis Station is situated on the A4086. Should you come by bus it will drop you near the station.

Entering Llanberis on the A4086 from the east, the Capel Curig side, you will see the Snowdon Mountain Railway on your left. There is a small car park in front of the station but this will soon fill up.

Arriving from the west, Caernarfon side, follow the A4086, which by passes the village. Go past the Electric Mountain visitor centre and the station is on your right.

The alternative parking places near here are: - Going towards Capel Curig, pass the station, take the first road right and there is a car park on the right.

Going towards Caernarfon. You can take first right marked Parc Padarn, there is a car park a few hundred yards down the road on the left.

Alternatively go straight on until you pass the Electric Mountain visitor centre. Take first right into the village coach and car park.

Opening Times & Details

The railway is open from mid March to the end of October. Depending on the weather conditions services may be curtailed.

Details from: Snowdon Mountain Railway, Llanberis, Gwynedd. LL55 4TY.

TALYLLYN RAILWAY
RHEILFFORDD TALYLLYN

The Talyllyn Railway is situated at Tywyn, in Gwynedd near Aberdyfi, the old spelling being Towyn. The line was built to carry slate from the Bryn Eglws quarry, which is in the mountain east of Abergynolwyn. The line was constructed from the Cambrian Railways at Tywyn to Abergynolwyn in 1865 to a gauge of 2'-3" the same gauge as the Corris Railway.

From Abergynolwyn to Nant Gwernol it was made as a light tramway. The locomotives worked this section for slate traffic only. The slate was brought down to Nant Gwernol by rope worked inclines. Before the line was constructed the slate had to be carried by packhorse to Aberdyfi for transport by sea.

The railway started to carry passengers over the winter of 1866/7. Sir Henry Haydn Jones, a business man from Tywyn acquired the railway with the quarries in 1911. Though the quarry closed in 1946, he kept it open, subsidising it at his own expense until his death in 1950. Luckily a preservation society was formed to keep the line running, this was the first line to be run by a preservation society. They had trains running the next spring to Rhydyronen and by summer to Abergynolwyn (6½ miles). The preservation society aimed to extend the line from Abergynolwyn to Nant Gwernol over the old tramway. The route had to be widened and a lot of effort put into the project. In 1976 the line was opened for passenger traffic, a total of 7¼ miles.

In the 1920's the G.W.R. used to advertise a round trip from Machynlleth, taking the train to Towyn and then by the Talyllyn Railway to Abergynolwyn. The passenger could then ride or walk the two miles to the Corris Railway, and travel by it to Machynlleth. Today at peak season you can take the train to Abergynolwyn and then take a bus via the Dyfi valley back to Tywyn.

The locomotives used on the line include the original ones.

No 1 Talyllyn built in 1864 as a 0-4-0ST. It was found not satisfactory for the line and was converted to a 0-4-2 ST in 1867. The locomotive has been rebuilt and modified several times.

No 2 Dolgoch built in 1866 0-4-0T.

No 3 & 4 are ex Corris Railway locomotives.

No 3 Sir Haydn built 1878 0-4-2 ST.

No 4 Edward Thomas built 1921 0-4-2 ST.

No 6 Douglas built in 1918 0-4-0T originally built for 2 foot gauge.

No 7 Tom Rolt was built by

Peter Sam (No 4 Edward Thomas) at Wharf Station, Tywyn — starting point for passengers on the Talyllyn Railway.

94

the T.R. in 1991 using parts from a locomotive built in 1948 it is a 0-4-2T.

All the locomotives are coal fired. The railway also has three diesel locomotives that are normally used on maintenance work.

Some of the original coaches also survived. Additional coaches have come from the Corris Railway, Penrhyn Quarry Railway and Glyn Valley Tramway. A lot of work has been done to some of these coaches and full details can be obtained in the Talyllyn Railway Handbooks. The railway has also built some of its own coaches. The doors of the coaches are all on one side as all the platforms are on the north side of the line. This has allowed for the fitting of storage heaters in one set of coaches for cold weather use. The heaters are charged up at night and keep the coaches warm during the daytime. Some of the coaches will take wheelchairs but should you need these facilities it is best to check with the railway before coming.

WHARF STATION TYWYN
Tywyn (Sand Dunes)
(The mileage shown is from this station which is at 40 feet above sea level)

At the station there is wheelchair access to the platform. There is a booking office and large shop. There is a public telephone at the station. Gentlemen, ladies and disabled toilets. At the end of the platform there is a cafe where you can enjoy a meal, in fine weather you can sit outside. At the station there is also a museum which is well worth a visit. This contains locomotives, rolling stock and many items of narrow gauge interest.

When you board the train you will notice that the locomotives usually have their front facing away from Tywyn so a good photograph may be taken from the main road over bridge. As the train climbs up the valley the best views can be seen from the platform side. Before you leave the guard will check your tickets. Should you want to get off at any of the halts please let him know. You can also buy your tickets from the guard should you get on at an unmanned station or halt.

How to Get There
The station is at the side of the A493. From Dolgellau follow the road through Tywyn past the B.R. Station, Wharf station is on your right.

From Aberdyfi go past the Hospital and Wharf station will be on your left after crossing the railway. There is no parking in front of the station, if you take the road in front of the station and cross over the B.R. rail bridge you will see a large car park on your right.

Wharf Station is ¼ mile south of Tywyn B.R. Station and is alongside the B.R. line.

Coming by train from Machynlleth direction, when you get off the train walk along the road on your left, cross over the railway bridge at the end of the road and Wharf station is on your right. From the Barmouth direction, walk to the main road turn right and follow the road, you will come to Wharf station on your right.

After the train leaves Wharf Station it goes under the main road, after a short distance you pass under another road bridge, this was the old turnpike road. Your train now enters the area of the Talyllyn workshops. A carriage shed, engine shed and works is on your right and there is also a carriage shed on your left. You will notice the small signal box on your right against the carriage shed. Here is a passing point and the driver will exchange the token for the Wharf section for the section from Pendre east. The train will pull into Pendre Station.

PENDRE STATION
(Top or end of the town)
(¼ mile/43 feet)

Pendre Station is situated on a minor road. The station has only a small waiting room and the rear coaches are usually off the platform. The guard will open the crossing gates and then the train will pull forward. It will stop clear of the crossing while the guard shuts the gates and boards the train.

How to Get There

Should you come by car there is only parking in the lane, which is very restricted, so take your car and park near Wharf Station. Coming into Tywyn on the A493 from Dolgellau after passing the cemetery take the first road on the left, then first left and the level crossing is in front of you.

HENDY HALT
(Old House)
(1 mile/60 feet)

After passing under the next road bridge you will enter the Snowdonia National Park. You pass a small industrial estate on you left and arrive at Hendy Halt. This halt is for private use of the nearby farm. The line then passes under another road bridge and shortly you will come to the next halt.

FACH GOCH HALT
(Red Nook)
(1½ miles/70 feet)

This is another private halt and is for use of the Farm Fach Goch that you will see on your right. After passing the halt the train proceeds up a gradient of 1: 229 then a 1: 77 climb passing under the next road bridge where you can see the next halt. You will have to be quick, as the platform is very short

CYNFAL HALT
(1¾ mile/91 feet)

This halt is just off the road leading to the farm. It is very narrow with no parking space, however it may be of use to walkers.

How to Get There

To get to the platform you will have to enter the field on the southeast side of the railway bridge and walk to the line to cross over it. This is not recommended. It is better to use the next station up the line.

RHYDYRONEN
(Ashford)
(2 miles/100 feet)

There is a shelter at the station. As the train leaves Rhydyronen the train climbs a 1:95 gradient until the line crosses the stream then there is a downhill section of 1:162 for a short distance. This is the only down hill section after leaving Tywyn to the end of the line.

How to Get There

To get to the station take the A493 from Tywyn in the Dolgellau direction until you come to the B4405. After about 100 yds when this road takes a left hand bend, carry straight on keeping to the left at the next junction. This will bring you to the station.

TYNLLWYN HALT
(Small holding by a grove)
(2½ miles/102 feet)
The halt is for the nearby farm of Tynllwyn Hen (Old House in Grove) and you will see the house on your right. There is a track leading to the halt from the B4405. The train will now start to climb up the valley and you will notice the main road running parallel to you on the lefthand side.

BRYNGLAS
(Hill of blue)
(3¼ miles/124 feet)
At the station there is a siding and a passing loop with a signal box. It is normally only used in peak season. There is a small shelter. The platform is to the east of the loop so when two trains pass an unusual working occurs. The up train will have to wait in the loop until the down train has left the platform and entered the loop and given his token to the signalman. Once the driver has received the token the up train can move forward to the platform. On leaving the station the train will carry on climbing until you cross the viaduct just before Dolgoch station.

How to Get There
To get to the station take the A493 from Tywyn in the Dolgellau direction until you come to the B4405. The road shortly takes a left hand bend, follow the B4405 for about ¼ mile and you come to a minor road on your right. Follow this road for 1 mile and you will come to the station. There is a small car parking area.

DOLGOCH
(Red Meadow)
(4¾ miles/187 feet)
Dolgoch station has a small shelter and new toilets are being built. The railway has had to go to the expense of putting in disabled facilities, when the only way you can get to the station in a wheelchair is by train. Both paths from the station have steep steps.

Before the train leaves the locomotive may take on water. Leaving Dolgoch the train has to climb a 1:76 gradient. Soon you will be at the next halt.

From the station you can walk to some spectacular waterfalls. You will need strong footwear to walk up to the falls. Leave the train and walk up the path on the left, and cross the railway by the footbridge. You will join the path from the car park. The lower falls are only a few minutes walk from the station. It will take at least an hour for the more energetic to walk to the head of the gorge.

To get to the car park take the path on the left going down and follow it down the steps.

How to Get There

The car park for the falls and station is in front of the Dolgoch Falls Hotel, on the bend by the side of the B4405. From here the path is marked for the Falls and Station. A splendid view of the three arch viaduct that is over 50ft above the stream can be seen from the path.

QUARRY SIDING
(5¼ miles/202 feet)

Quarry siding station is just off the B4405. There is a passing loop and a signal box where the token could be exchanged. The overgrown quarry here was once used to supply ballast for the railway. As the train proceeds from here to Abergynolwyn you will notice some of the old slate fencing used by the railway. New fencing has had to be put in some places and you will notice that the wire mesh is green to blend in with the background.

ABERGYNOLWYN
(Mouth of the river with whirlpool)
(6½ miles/243 feet)

Should the electric light signals be set at clear your train will enter the station and you will pass the down train on the right. Your train will then pull into the platform and stop with the locomotive by the signal box. The platform has to accommodate two full trains, and allow room for the points from the loop line, so at 620 feet it is the longest narrow gauge platform in Wales.

One of the train crew will now have to go to the signal box and hand in the token for the down section and pick up the token for the Nant Gwernol section. Do not get off your train, as it will soon proceed to Nant Gwernol.

When only one train is operating the signal box is usually unmanned. Your train will enter the station on the platform line and continue to the signal box. The crew will then exchange the tokens and proceed to Nant Gwernol.

The station also has a booking office. Should this be unmanned you can get your ticket from the guard. It is very nice to take the train from here. Arrive in good time and have a meal in the cafe. Then take the train to Tywyn, spend time there and come back by a later train.

How to Get There
The station entrance is just off the B4405 on the left just over ½ mile on

the Tywyn side of Abergynolwyn. Go along the road and the car park is on the right. There are toilets in the car park and also on the station. You can get from the car park to the station by following the road up to the station. On foot there is a short cut up the steps next to the disabled toilet. Next to the car park is a picnic area.

NANT GWERNOL
(Alder Stream)
(7¾ miles/269 feet)
The line from Abergynolwyn follows the old tramway line. Shortly after leaving the station the train will go over the forestry road level crossing. You will then be able to see the village of Abergynolwyn on your left on the floor of the valley. You may be able to make out the old incline. This was used to send goods down

An expressive view of Talyllyn Railway's Peter Sam at Nant Gwernol. Having arrived from Tywyn, the engine will soon run round the train.

from the railway to the village. The train swings to the right towards Nant Gwernol station where there is a small waiting room. You are now at the end of the line and the locomotive will run round the train before going back to Abergynolwyn.

There is no road access to the station. There is a footpath from the village, and you can walk up to the old inclines. You can also walk through the forestry paths back to Abergynolwyn station. There is a leaflet available for walks from the station. Ask at the station when you get your tickets or ask the guard.

RETURN TO ABERGYNOLWYN
On the return journey the train will stop at the signal box to drop off one of the crew to return the token for the Nant Gwernol section, then proceed all the way down the platform to the West End. Should only one train be in service it will stop nearly opposite the cafe so the crew does not have as far to walk, when they are ready to depart.

The train will now wait for about 30 minutes until the up train has arrived, this gives you time to visit the shop and cafe. You can also sit outside the cafe on the station platform. On the side of the platform is a display of original Talyllyn point work. After the up train has arrived the crew will obtain the token from the signal box for the down section, and will have to walk the full length of the platform.

Opening Times & Details
The round trip takes about 2½ hours. The railway operates a Sunday service mid February to about Easter then daily to the end of October. There are special services at Christmas.

Details from: Talyllyn Railway, Wharf Station, Tywyn, Gwynedd. LL36 9EY.

VALE OF RHEIDOL RAILWAY
The line was opened in 1902 up the Cwm Rheidol (Rheidol Valley) with a gauge of 1'-11¾". It was to carry passengers, timber from the forests, lead, silver and ore from the mines to the harbour at Aberystwyth. In Aberystwyth the line followed a different route from that used today. It ran from the harbour, following the Rheidol to the area near Ysgol Plascrug/ Plascrug School. At Plascrug there were exchange sidings with the main line. The

original station was at right angles to Coedlan y Parc/Park Avenue, on the south side, next to where the Bus Depot is today. The line was amalgamated with the Cambrian Railways in 1913, and was absorbed by the G.W.R. in 1922.

The branch to the harbour was closed in 1924 and lifted in 1930. In 1927 a new terminus was built by the G.W.R. alongside the main station, extending the line just under a ¼ mile. They also introduced new locomotives, built at Swindon, and new coaching stock. The line could not take a direct route out of the new station as it had to pass under the main line that went to Lampeter and Carmarthen.

The line was closed from 1940 to 1945, and passed to British Railways Western Region in 1948, becoming part of the London Midland Region in 1963. After the closing of the Lampeter and Carmarthen line it was realigned from the station to beyond the old Plascrug sidings, giving a more direct run from the station. The line was the last to run steam locomotives on British Railways. In 1989 it was privatised and is now run by the company that operates the Brecon Mountain Railway at Merthyr Tydfil.

During British Railway ownership the loop at Aberffrwd was removed. This meant that at peak times the trains had to leave Aberystwyth one behind the other. Once all the trains were at Devil's Bridge they would follow each other back down the line. This meant that there was a long time between the first three trains from Aberystwyth and the next three. With the line now under control of Brecon Mountain Railway the loop has been reinstated and a more practical timetable can be operated.

The original locomotives used on the line were No1 Edward VII 2-6-2T 1902 (renumbered by the G.W.R. 1212 and scrapped in 1935)

No 2 Prince of Wales 2-6-2T 1902 (G.W.R. No 1213) this was heavily rebuilt by the G.W.R. in 1924 into what amounted to a new locomotive, becoming B.R. No 9.

The third locomotive was No 3 Rheidol 2-4-0T built in 1896 and obtained from the contractor who built the line. (G.W.R. No 1198, and scrapped in 1924)

In 1923 the G.W.R. built at Swindon, two locomotives based on No 2. Both were 2-6-2T but more powerful and eventually named by B.R. in 1954, No 7 Owain Glyndwr, and No 8 Llywelyn, they weighed 25 tons each.

All the locomotives have been converted to oil firing to reduce the fire risk in the forestry section. The locomotives face in the Devil's Bridge direction.

The line now has a diesel locomotive No 10 built in 1987 by the Brecon Mountain Railway Company for British Rail.

The coaches are 4 observation built in 1923 and 12 closed built in 1937/8, but all have been refurbished, and are now air braked. There is first class accommodation in coaches with guard's compartment. Most of the coaches are fully enclosed but there are a few unglazed coaches for summer use. There is limited space for wheelchairs.

ABERYSTWYTH
(Mouth of the river Ystwyth/flexible)
(0 miles/14 feet)

The measurements for the line are in miles from here and the height of the stations is above sea level

The line shares the station with the standard gauge line. The Vale of Rheidol platform is at the south side of the station. Each railway has its own booking office.

At the station there is a ramp down to the platform that is on a level with the railway lines. For the best views further up the valley sit on the left hand side which is nearest the main line. The guard will check your tickets before the train leaves. As the train departs you will see the old main line shed on your left now occupied by the railway. In the yard you can see various types of maintenance wagons. You will see the river come towards the line on the right. This is the area where the old exchange sidings were. Your train will soon reach Llanbadarn.

How to Get There
Arriving by train you will see the terminus on your left as you arrive. Get off the train and walk along the platform to the booking office and shop for the railway.

Coming by bus you will get off on the north side of the station. Walk along Ffordd Alexandra/Alexandra Road in the direction of the traffic, past the front of the station, turn left and walk straight on. The V.o.R booking office and shop is in front of you.

By road from the north on the A487 follow the one way system and you will be directed past the station along Ffordd Alexandra/Alexandra

Road. Continue to the roundabout and turn left into Coedlan y Parc/Park Avenue. You will find plenty of car parks along this road.

From the south on the A487, after crossing the Rheidol Bridge turn first right into Dan Dre/Mill Street. At the roundabout turn right into Coedlan y Parc/Park Avenue. You will find plenty of car parks along this road.

From the car parks you will be able to see the station. The V.o.R booking office and shop is on this side of the station.

LLANBADARN
(1¼ miles/16 feet)

This is a halt on the left of the line by the side of the A4120. One of the train crew will push the plunger to operate the lights for the road crossing. As the train crosses the road you will notice on your left, that the main line has its own crossing. Shortly afterwards you cross over the Rheidol by the Black Bridge. This timber bridge has had a lot of repair work carried out on it since Brecon Railway took over the line. Looking to your left, you will see the main line swing away to the north on the other side of the Rheidol. Your train will now stay on the south side of the Rheidol for the rest of its journey. Following the river you will see a road bridge over it and you will go over a level crossing. On your left is the old road, and on the right an industrial estate. At the other end of the estate the old road crosses the line and you come to the next halt.

GLANRAFON
(Bank of the river)
(2¼ miles/31 feet)

This is a halt by the side of the old road crossing. The line now follows the river keeping to the valley floor. You will see the old road on your right until you reach Capel Bangor.

CAPEL BANGOR
(Chapel Bangor)
(4½ miles/75 feet)

The halt has a shelter and is on the right hand side of the line just before the level crossing. The line has been nearly level all the way from Aberystwyth and has climbed to only 66 feet, in the 20 minutes it has taken you to get to Capel Bangor. From the station it starts the climb from the valley bottom. Devil's Bridge is at 680 feet, so the train will have to climb 78 feet up for every mile it travels.

NANTYRONEN
(Stream of the Ronen)
(6¾ miles/197 feet)

The halt is situated just after the road crossing, and your train will stop to take on water for the rest of the climb. Once the tank has been topped up your train will leave and climb the 1:48 incline just outside the station. You may be able to see some old mine workings on your left.

ABERFFRWD
(Mouth of the stream)
(7¾ miles/253 feet)

At the station is the reinstated passing loop. The train crew operates the points and lights at the loop. The down train usually arrives first, and draws into the loop. A member of the crew sets the points and signals for the up train. When it has arrived the points are reset behind it for the down train to proceed. After your train has pulled out of the loop it will stop while one of the train crew resets the points ready for your return.

As your train crosses over the last level crossing, you will notice the steep gradient of the road at this point. Your train will now carry on up the valley, most of the line being on a gradient of 1:50. Most of the track is on a ledge that has been cut out of the side of the valley. You will proceed round a horseshoe bend and towards the dam across the river. Look to the left across the valley and you will see the Rheidol Stag. This has been made by the tipping of mine spoil from a tramway that ran along the back of it. Further on you will see on the other side of the river the Hydro Power Station which is run by Power Gen. The water to feed the power station comes from the Nant-y-Moch reservoir high in the mountain behind.

RHEIDOL FALLS
(9¾ miles/425 feet)

This halt has no road access though there is a footpath. As the train leaves look over the valley to the Rheidol Falls, if it has been wet you will see the cascade on hillside. About ½ mile after leaving the Halt you enter another large horseshoe bend. You can see your locomotive working hard up the gradient on the ledge.

RHIWFRON
(Hill by the river)
(10¾ miles/542 feet)

One of the sturdy engines on the Vale of Rheidol line between Aberystwyth and Devil's Bridge is the No 8 Llewelyn, 2-6-2T, built by GWR at Swindon in 1923.

This halt also has no road access but a track comes near to the halt. A footpath crosses the line at this point. From here you can see across the valley the Cwmrheidol mine. The lead ore from the mine used to be carried by an aerial rope way across the valley to a siding at the halt. The train continues up the valley finally entering Devil's Bridge through a rock cutting.

DEVIL'S BRIDGE
(Pontarfynach)
(11¾ miles/639 feet)

At the station is a cafe with shop, and toilets. The train will wait here about 45 minutes but check the timetable.

A short walk away is Devil's Bridge and falls. To get to them go through the car park on to the road and turn left. Devil's Bridge and falls is on the right.

How to Get There
The car park is situated alongside the A4120.

Opening Times & Details
The journeys takes one hour each way, allow 3 hours for round trip.

The railway operates from Easter to the end of October with restricted services in early and late season.

Details from: Vale of Rheidol Railway, Park Avenue, Aberystwyth. Ceredigion. SY23 1PG.

WELSH HIGHLAND RAILWAY CAERNARFON

The new line of the Welsh Highland Railway started to be laid in 1997 from Caernarfon to Dinas. It is laid partly on the standard gauge track bed, which ran from the junction at Menai Bridge near Bangor to Afon Wen in the South.

The Bangor and Caernarvon railway built the north section in 1852. The line was the first of three standard gauge lines to Caernarfon. This line was single track with passing points but was made into double track after a few years. When the line was due for closing it had a short burst of life due to the fire on the Britannia Bridge in May 1970. The Irish cattle boats used Caernarfon instead of Holyhead until the bridge was reopened in January 1972. The line was closed by British Railways in 1972.

The Caernarvon and Portmadoc railway constructed the southern section (The English spelling being used on the original railways.) The line joined up with the Cambrian Coast line at Afon Wen and was opened in 1867. A third line from the town, the Caernarvon and Lanberis railway was opened in 1869 and departed from the quay. Both these lines were single track with passing places.

All the three lines were to become part of the L.N.W.R. A station was built at the north end of the town. From the station two single lines left the station, one for Afon Wen and the other for Llanberis. The railway went through a tunnel under Castle Square, the tracks splitting just before reaching the main A487 road. The Llanberis line followed the north bank of the Seiont. The Afon Wen line crossed it by a bridge and headed towards Dinas. The line south from Caernarfon followed approximately the old Nantlle railway track bed. This line had been constructed in 1828 to a gauge of 3'-6", from Nantlle to the quay at Caernarfon. In 1867 the section of the Nantlle railway between Caernarfon and Penygroes was converted to standard gauge and some of the curves on the old narrow gauge railway were eased out. Regular passenger working stopped on the Llanberis line in 1930 but excursion trains still ran until the line finally closed in 1964. The Caernarfon Avon Wen line closed in 1963.

The new line starts from a new station, which is after the tunnel, where the track bed had carried two standard gauge tracks. There had been proposals to build a station with an island platform near here when the standard gauge line was in use. The line is run by the Ffestiniog Railway and has the same gauge of 1'-11½". The line runs to Dinas, a distance of 3 miles. Allow about one hour for your visit and ride.

The steam locomotives used on this line are NGG16 Garratts 2-6-2+2-6-2 from South African Railways and are oil fired. When work has been completed there will also be a large diesel locomotive built in South Africa by Funkey. These will be supplemented as required by locomotives from the Ffestiniog fleet. The locomotives usually travel with the boiler facing Dinas.

Winston Engineering has made the new 1997 coaching stock, which have inward opening doors, and are comfortable. The coaches that have guards vans have been constructed with wide doors to take wheelchairs. There is a corridor between coaches. The coaches are heated for cold weather and have electric lighting. There are also coaches for use in fine weather, which have unglazed windows. Pullman first class carriages are being constructed which will be used for wine and dine trains. The new coaches are built to a wider loading gauge than the Ffestiniog stock so will not be able to operate on the Ffestiniog line.

Beyer Garratt near St Helen's Road bridge on the Welsh Highland Railway, Caernarfon.

CAERNARFON STATION
(Fort of Arfon)

The station is in St Helen's Road. The new narrow gauge station has one platform, which is accessible to wheelchairs. There is a temporary booking office. The line has a short head shunt and a run round loop for the locomotive. The line leaves for the south and runs alongside St Helens's Road. Since the lifting of the standard gauge line the trackbed had become a cycle track. Just after leaving the station this cycle track joins the railway on the right hand side. It will follow the line all the way to Dinas.

In places the track bed was too narrow to take both the new railway and cycle track, and the cycle track has been diverted on a new course for short distances. Using this track it is ideal to get close up photographs of the train without trespassing onto railway property. The tracks along St Helen's Road are best for the sun in the morning and south of here the sun is in the correct direction in the afternoon.

Further on as St Helen's Road starts to rise our line bears right. On the left you can see where the old track for the

Llanberis branch went. Just over a mile from Caernarfon the train will have to stop at a minor road junction to check the road is clear before proceeding. As the train enters Dinas station you will see the yard on your left-hand side with the present shed.

How to Get There

Coming by bus get off at the bus station in Penllyn, walk to the traffic lights and turn left into Bridge Street. Follow the road to Castle Square, go past the Post Office and turn left into Segontium Terrace. The railway can be seen over the wall on the right. Follow the wall until you come to the bridge over the railway and cross over to the station.

If you have a wheelchair follow the Square round to the castle and turn left down the road to the quay. Take first left into St Helen's Road, the station is on the left hand side. It is proposed to build a road through the old tunnel. Work has already started at the north end up to the tunnel mouth. Until work is completed there is a small car park between the old tunnel entrance and the station. Should this be full then there is a large car and coach park on the quayside.

To get to the station from the A487.

Coming from the south, as the road enters Caernarfon there is a roundabout. Take the left hand road signpost for the castle. This is St Helen's Road. You will straight away cross over the railway on a new bridge, follow the road and the station is on your right hand side.

From the Bangor direction to avoid the town centre follow the signs on the A487 for Porthmadog. Go over the flyover and into a small one way system.*

From Llanberis on the A4086 you will pass the fire station on your right, and come to a roundabout. Take the first exit marked for Porthmadog (A487). Continue to the next roundabout and take the first exit for Porthmadog (A487) this will bring you to the one way system*.

The A4085 from Beddgelert leads straight into the one way system*.

*From the one way system take the road marked A487 Porthmadog. You will pass a petrol station on the left and come to a roundabout. Take the right hand turn signpost for the castle. This is St Helen's Road. You will straight away cross over the railway on a new bridge, follow the road and the station is on your right hand side.

Should you want the Tourist Information Centre it is in Castle Ditch. From Castle Square follow the road alongside the Castle, keeping the Castle on your left. This is Castle Ditch; the Centre is on the right of the road almost opposite the Castle entrance.

Passengers at Dinas station admire the Welsh Highland Railway's 2-6-2 + 2-6-2, NGG16 Beyer Garratt.

Other attractions in Caernarfon are the Castle, Maritime Museum near Victory Dock. The Roman Museum is in Llanbeblig Road. This is on the road leading to Beddgelert.

To get there from Castle Square on foot, go up Pool Street across the A487 into Tithebarn Street and carry straight on into Constantine Road and Llanbeblig Road. The Museum is on the left, about ½ mile from Castle Square.

DINAS
(Fort or camp)

The station has two platforms and will be a passing point when the line is extended. Until then it will be used as a run round loop for the locomotives. When the train arrives, the locomotive will be uncoupled and run forward. It will then take on water if required. The old narrow gauge yard is beyond the bridge. The present line uses the right hand side of the bridge, which used to be for the standard gauge line. The old narrow gauge line used to use the left-hand side, which has at present a roadway through it to the yard.

111

The standard gauge line carried straight on towards Afon Wen. After the goods yard the narrow gauge line turned off left towards a road bridge to go under the A487. The North Wales Narrow Gauge Railways originally built this line from Dinas to Rhyd Ddu, being opened in stages between 1877 and 1881. The line from Rhyd Ddu was eventually extended and became Welsh Highland Railway. This line then ran from Dinas to Beddgelert and on to Porthmadog.

It is proposed to extend the new narrow gauge line from Dinas on the alignment of the old Welsh Highland Railway line to Porthmadog.

The station is on the level and is accessible to wheelchairs, it will have a booking office and shop with facilities for light refreshments. Toilets will include ladies, gentlemen's and disabled

How to Get There

The station is off the A487. From the roundabout where the A499 from Pwllheli joins the A487 from Porthmadog, follow the road towards Caernarfon, for about ¼ mile. On the left is a road signpost to Saron and Dinas.

From Caernarfon follow the A487 through Bontnewydd till you come to Dinas. Shortly after entering the 40mph zone you will see the sign for Saron and Dinas. Turn right.

After turning into the Sharon and Dinas road turn first right and keep to the left lane. The entrance to the car park is at the bottom on the right.

The car park will not hold a great number of cars yet, but it is hoped it can be extended. Should you be coming by car to ride on the line it is advisable to go to Caernarfon.

Opening Times & Details

The railway will be open from Easter to the end of October.

The line is operated by the Ffestiniog Railway. Details from: Ffestiniog Railway, Harbour Station, Porthmadog. Gwynedd. LL49 9NF.

WELSH HIGHLAND RAILWAY PORTHMADOG
RHEILFFORDD UCHELDIR CYMRU

The history of this line has been well documented and a book is on sale at the shop. The Welsh Highland Railway line was the combination of several lines. The North Wales Narrow Gauge Railway from Dinas to Rhyd Ddu was built between 1877 and 1881. The Croesor Tramway (built in 1864) and The Gorsedd Junction and Portmadoc Railway connected with the Croesor Tramway. In 1901 the Portmadoc Beddgelert & South Snowdon Railway was formed, but they only did some earth works. (The English spelling was used on the original railways.)

In 1923 work was completed on a line from Rhyd Ddu through Beddgelert to the Croesor Tramway. It was named The Welsh Highland Railway. By 1934 the Ffestiniog Railway leased the line. Passenger services finished in 1936 and goods in 1937. Some of the track was lifted for the war efforts in 1941 and stock sold in 1942.

The section from Porthmadog to Croesor junction had been left in place but with the decline of the slate traffic the sections, which were still in place, were lifted in 1948.

Part of the present car park was originally the trackbed of the Gorsedda line, which ran through where there is a footpath now and where it now crosses the main line by a stile. This track bed can be followed part of the way towards the harbour. When the Cambrian Railways came to Porthmadog the area held the cattle pens for the main line. A track also ran alongside the standard gauge line, past the present sheds to a transfer siding called Beddgelert Sidings. The narrow gauge line follows very near to this formation.

The locomotives used on the line are larger than the types used in the quarries. The main locomotives, which are coal-fired steam:- Russell 2-6-2T built in 1906 used to work on the Welsh Highland Railway.

Karen 0-4-2T built 1942 worked in Rhodesia.

Gelert 0-4-2T built 1953 came from Johannesburg.

Moel Tryfan 0-4-2T built 1953 and Pedemoura 0-6-0WT built 1924.

The diesels include 3 ex Polish State Forests. They are 0-6-0, which are Diesel Hydraulic built 1980 in Romania. There is also a selection of small diesel locomotives. The passenger coaches include an observation and brake, semi-open and open toast rack. There are also the original North Wales Narrow Gauge coaches that are fully glazed, one has been modified into a buffet car, and the Gladstone Car.

The line has a gauge of 1'-11½", the same as the Ffestiniog railway. The signals on the line are semaphore type. They are hand operated or semi automatic worked by electric motors. Cab or footplate rides sometimes can be made. If you would like one enquire in the shop.

PORTHMADOG STATION

From the car park there is a level path to the shop and a ramp to the cafe, which serves both hot and cold snacks. There are toilets on site and in 1998 the railway should open a disabled toilet. Wheelchair passengers can be taken on the train but it means them having to be lifted on and off. Please therefore contact the railway before arriving so that they can make suitable arrangements.

At the station there is a run round loop for the locomotive. Before your train leaves one of the crew will contact the shop to make sure there are no late passengers. Then they operate the signal controls and the train can depart. The train will go to Pen y Mount Halt passing the locomotive and carriage sheds on your right hand side.

How to Get There

The Station is situated on the A487 opposite the Porthmadog British Rail Station. From the British rail station the entrance is on the left across the main road.

Coming by road from the Caernarfon direction on the A487 follow the road through Tremadog. After entering Porthmadog the entrance is on the left just before the level crossing. From the South go through Porthmadog on the A487, the entrance is on the right just after the level crossing.

From Criccieth on the A497 follow the road in to Porthmadoc, bear left at the roundabout and follow the A487. The entrance is on the right just after the level crossing.

PEN Y MOUNT HALT

This station has been constructed to look like a Welsh Highland Station in 1922 with a shelter. The locomotive will run round your train and return along the line.

114

LOCOMOTIVE SHED

On the return journey the train will normally stop at the locomotive shed and you will be invited to look round.

The run is approximately ¾ mile long. Allow about one hour for your visit.

Opening Times & Details

The railway normally operates from Easter, weekends and Bank holidays until June then daily till the end of September. Then weekend and the school half term in October.

Details from: The Welsh Highland Railway Centre, Tremadog Road, Porthmadog. LL49 9HP.

WELSHPOOL & LLANFAIR RAILWAY

The beginnings of the railway can be traced to a horse worked line that ran from a quarry near Raven Square to the canal in the town centre, though this was closed by 1854. The Oswestry and Newtown Railway, that later became part of the Cambrian Railways, came to Welshpool in 1860. There were several proposals to build a line up the valley to serve the farms and villages in the valleys between Welshpool (Y Trallwng) and Llanfair Caereinion.

The Welshpool & Llanfair Light Railway Company eventually built the line. It was opened in 1903 and was 9 miles long, built to a gauge of 2'-6". The line was operated by the Cambrian Railways and ran from their station in Welshpool. The G.W.R. closed the line to passenger traffic in 1931 and British Railways to goods in 1956.

A group of enthusiasts came together in 1960 and formed a company to take over the line. It was the first time a preservation group had taken over a line from British Railways. The first section was opened in 1963 from Llanfair Caereinion to Castle Caereinion. However the bridge over the River Banwy was damaged by storms in December 1964. This was repaired and services resumed in August 1965. The line to Sylfaen opened in 1972 and to Raven Square, Welshpool in 1981. Beyond this the line ran through the town. In1963 the enthusiasts managed to work a train over this section before it was lifted. You can still walk some of the route but in some places it has changed greatly in appearance, as part of it went through the Bron-y-Buckley

115

housing estate.

The locomotives now used on the line are coal fired steam ones and include the original two No 1 The Earl and No 2 The Countess built in 1902 0-6-0T. The British Railways numbers for these locomotives were 822 & 823

Other locomotives have been imported to the line.

No 6 Monarch built 1953 0-4-4-0T

No 8 Dougal built 1946 0-4-0T

No 10 Sir Drefaldwyn built 1944 0-8-0TT

No 12 Joan built 1927 0-6-2T

No 14 built 1954 2-6-2T

No 15 Orion built 1948 2-6-2T

They normally face in the Llanfair direction. The line also has some diesel locomotives, which can be used on passenger and work trains. The main one for passenger use is No 7 Chattenden built 1949. It is a six coupled 150 H.P. locomotive.

None of the original coaches survived to be used on the line. The coaches now in use have come from various places including Zillertalbahn in Austria and West Africa. The older ones date from 1900 and newer ones from 1961. A lot of work has been

The Welshpool and Llanfair Railway's No 10, 0–8–0T Sir Drefaldwyn at Llanfair station.

Contrast in size as Welshpool and Llanfair railway's 0-6-0T The Countess dwarfs No 8 0-4-0T Dougal outside Llanfair engine shed.

carried out over the years and some of them have been adapted to carry wheelchairs.

LLANFAIR CAEREINION
(450 feet)

The station at Llanfair Caereinion is the main terminus of the line. The station has a shop, cafe and a booking office. There are gentleman's and ladies toilets at the station. Work is in progress to upgrade the station. There is only one platform and you will step up onto the coaches. Ramps can be provided for wheelchairs at both here and at Raven Square.

The line is single track with passing loops. The driver will obtain the staff for the section before you leave and as the train draws out you will notice the semaphore signals and the signal box on the left. Your train will pass the engine sheds and workshop on your right and then the carriage sheds. You will soon see the river on your right and pass the old mill on your left.

How to Get There

The station is situated alongside the A458 road on the Welshpool side of the village. There is a coach and car park behind the station. There are ramps on the paths to the station for wheelchairs.

HENIARTH GATE
(1½ miles)

The first station is Heniarth Gate, it is just a grass strip. Your train will shortly cross over and follow the River Banwy. Your train now crosses the Cwmbaw stream on the Brynelin viaduct, that is 350 feet above sea level. The river goes down the valley on your left to eventually join the River Severn. The train now starts the climb to Castle Caereinion.

CYFRONYDD
(2¼ miles)

Soon your train will stop and one of the crew will go forward to open the crossing gates. The train will then proceed into Cyfronydd station. Look on your left, and you will notice that the gates are not across the road as they are there only to protect the line. The guard will shut the gates after the train has passed. The station has a loop line and a small platform. There is a shed with a small veranda.

How to Get There

Cyfronydd Station is on a minor road near the church just off the A458.

DOLARDDYN CROSSING
(3½ miles)

The train will now continue to Dolarddyn Crossing and will stop. One of the crew goes forward with a flag to the open level crossing. The train will then proceed up the 1:32 incline.

CASTLE CAEREINION
(4¼ miles)

Just before reaching Castle Caereinion, there is one more stop for the crew to open the crossing gates. This time they are swung back until they are alongside the road, one on each side. Here there is a passing loop, waiting room and platform.

You will also be able to see the signal box. This box was

opened in 1907 and closed in 1931, but is now used again. Should you look back to Llanfair you will see some nice views. The village is only a short distance from the station. The train leaves on a climb of 1:46 up to Coppice Lane crossing which is the second highest point on the line. On the other side the line has a down gradient of 1:40. The line then starts to climb again.

How to Get There
The station is on the B4385.

SYLFAEN
(5¼ miles)

There is a passing loop and a waiting room. The line continues to climb until it reaches the highest point on the line, 603 feet above sea level, just before Golfa station.

How to Get There
The station is alongside the A458.

GOLFA
(6¼ miles)

The line drops down past another open level crossing to Golfa. There is now a mile long gradient of 1:29. Just before Raven Square you will cross the last open level crossing. The line from here has a gradient of 1:43, a test for the train as it leaves the station on its return journey.

RAVEN SQUARE WELSHPOOL
(8 Miles)

Raven Square is a single platform on your right with the signal box. The station has a large coach and car park with a picnic area. The main station building came from Eardisley Station in the Wye valley. In the building are a booking office, and a shop where you can get light snacks. There is also a small museum showing the history of the line. The toilet block was constructed to match the station with parts coming from Horninglow on the North Staffordshire Railway, it contains gentleman's, ladies and disabled toilets. There is also a waiting room on the platform.

How to Get There
Should you come by train, when you get off the train go up on to the

footbridge and turn right over the bridge. As you come off the bridge you are by a small car park. Stand with the old station on your left and the small roundabout on your right. Cross over the road into Severn Street and keep following this road to the end. You will cross the main road in the town centre into Broad Street, High Street, Chapel Street, Mount Street and Raven Street, which will bring you to Raven Square. There is a roundabout in the middle of the square and you will see the station on your left. It is about 1 mile from the Central Rail station to Raven Square.

Some bus services go past the station and others will drop you off in the town centre.

Coming from Oswestry on the A483, as you enter Welshpool take the A498 to the town centre then turn right at the traffic lights on to the A490 to Raven Square. From Newtown or Ludlow take the A490 to the town centre turn left at the traffic lights and follow it to Raven Square. From Llanfair Caereinion on the A458 you will see the station on your right as you approach Welshpool. The paths from the coach and car park are ramped for wheelchairs.

Opening Times & Details

A round trip Llanfair to Llanfair will take about 2¼ hours but check the timetable.

The railway is open from Easter to October. There is restricted opening early and late season except for the Bank Holidays. It is open every day mid July and August. There is also a restricted service in December. For details contact The Station, Llanfair Caereinion. Powys SY21 0SF.

3
CABLE HAULED LINES

ABERYSTWYTH ELECTRIC CLIFF RAILWAY

The Aberystwyth Cliff Railway is a funicular line. It runs up Constitution Hill and is stated to be the longest in Great Britain. It is 778ft long with a gauge of 4'-9". It was opened in 1896 and consists of two parallel tracks each with a carriage on it connected by a rope, which passes over a pulley at the top of the incline. The original carriages were worked by water. Each carriage had a 1000 gallon tank built into it. Water would be allowed to fill the top carriage until it started to move, this pulled the other carriage up. When the carriage reached the bottom it would then discharge its water. The water would be pumped up to the top into a reservoir to repeat the process. The water was pumped up using a steam driven pump.

To reduce the cost of operation in 1921 an electric motor was installed to operate the winding gear. The present owners took over in 1975 and more improvements have been made to the railway. A 55 HP (41KW) direct current motor now supplies the power through reduction gears. The carriages travel at 4 M.P.H. and stop precisely in the stations. The equipment can be controlled from either of the stations.

You will need to go up steps to get on the carriages. At the top there is a very nice cafe from which there are good views over the bay. The toilets are separate and are on the right after leaving the lift. A short walk to the top of the hill

The Lord Marks, one of the cars that climb Constitution Hill on the Aberystwyth Electric Cliff Railway.

brings you to the Camera Obscura. The original one was installed within a few years of the cliff railway being opened. The present one was built in 1985, and is designed to look like a Victorian building. The building is two storeys high and round the upper storey there is a balcony from which you can admire the scenery. The Camera Obscura is well worth a visit. On the table you will see Aberystwyth, and you can manipulate the lens to change the view. There is an excellent display of historical photographs and on the ground floor there is a small gift shop.

How to Get There

Constitution Hill is at the north end of the promenade in Aberystwyth. From the railway station's new entrance, turn right into the main road Ffordd Alexandra/Alexandra Road. Go straight across down Ffordd y M r/Terrace Road, until you reach the promenade. Turn right and walk along the promenade on Glan y M r/Marine Terrace, and Rhodfa Fuddug/Victoria Terrace. When you come to the end you will see the Cliff Railway Station up on the right.

Coming by road from the south on the A487, after crossing the Harbour bridge carry straight on into the one way system, Heol y Bont/Bridge Street. Though the one way system turns right at the end of this street you carry straight on down Heol y Wig/Pier Street to the promenade. Turn right along the promenade to the far end. You will then have to walk up to the Cliff Railway Station on the right. As parking is restricted on the promenade it might be advantageous to turn right into Maes Albert/Albert Place then turn left into Morfa Mawr/Queen's Road. The Cliff Railway Station is at the end of this road.

From the north on the A487 you will come down Ffordd Penglais/Penglais Road. After the junction with the A44 at the bottom of the hill, turn sharp right into Ffordd y Gogledd/North Road. Continue to the T junction, were you turn left into Coedlan y Frenhines/Queen's Avenue. Turn right into Morfa Mawr/Queen's Road. Follow this road and it will lead you to the Cliff Railway Station.

Opening Times & Details

The railway is open from Easter to the end of October.

Details from: Aberystwyth Electric Cliff Railway, Cliff Terrace, Aberystwyth, Ceredigion. SY23 2DN.

CENTRE FOR ALTERNATIVE TECHNOLOGY

The centre was started by a group of committed people who wanted to show how alternative technology could be used. The centre was set up on an old quarry site on the hillside near where the old Corris line used to run. The centre has added various forms of environmentally friendly displays. These help you to be aware of what can be done. They show how to produce electricity from solar cells, wind and water turbines and how to use energy efficiently and recycle waste. There is an adventure playground.

To get to the site from the car park there is a walk up the steep hill. To assist visitors to the site the centre installed a water balanced cliff railway. This was installed on part of the site where there used to be an incline from the quarry to get the slate down to the Corris Railway. The carriages run on a track with a gauge of 1.44m 5'-0¾", these being ex British Rail flat bottom rail. The track was laid on a longitudinal concrete bed. The line is 175 feet long and rises 100 feet. The two carriages can each carry up to 17 passengers and can accommodate wheelchairs.

The principal of operation is simple but requires a lot of equipment to make it work efficiently. At the top station there is

A step ride to the top of the water balanced cliff railway at the Centre of Alternative Technology, near Machynlleth.

a lake feed from a stream. The water is allowed into the carriage until the total weight is greater than the carriage at the bottom. The water supply is then cut off and when the brakes are released the top carriage is allowed to pull the bottom one up. The speed of the winding drum is controlled so that the carriages travel at about 1½ miles per hour and do not exceed the maximum speed. When the carriage reaches the bottom the water is discharged into a small reservoir at the bottom. This is also fed from the water that runs down the side of the road. The overflow comes out on the right hand side of the bottom station. The level of the lake at the top station is monitored. In dry weather should the level drop then water can be pumped up from the bottom reservoir. A computer is used to assist in the control of the whole railway operation. Because of the possibility of frozen water causing damage, and to allow for maintenance, the railway only operates from Easter to the end of October.

Both stations are designed to allow wheelchair access. The bottom station has gentleman's, ladies, and disabled toilets, these are repeated on the top site. Only Guide dogs are allowed on site. At the top there is a shop with a selection of books on various subjects including the environment. They also have a number of booklets on the different things that can be seen on the site. There is a cafe, which serves vegetarian lunches and picnic areas, some of which are under cover.

How to Get There
The Centre is located on the east side of the A487 about 3 miles north of Machynlleth. The lane to the site is well signposted, follow it and take first right, you will come to the coach and car park. The nearest Railway station is Machynlleth and bus services No 2, 30, & 34 operate to the end of the lane.

Opening Times & Details
The site is open all the year round, except over Christmas and part of January.

Details from: The Centre for Alternative Technology, Machynlleth, Powys. SY20 9AZ.

GREAT ORME TRAMWAY LLANDUDNO
The Great Orme Tramway runs from the Victoria Station in

Church Walks to near the summit of the Great Orme in two sections. The lower part was opened in 1902, up to Halfway, the top section being opened the next year in 1903. The gauge is 3'-6". The engine house is at Halfway Station. This was worked originally by a steam engine. In 1958 electric motors were installed to operate the line. The two sections are worked independently. The bottom section is 872yds and the top section 827yds long. Each of the sections has two passenger cars. The operators try to arrange that the top and bottom cars make a connection at Halfway.

VICTORIA STATION

The bottom section starts from Victoria Station, which is about 90 feet above sea level. Here there is a booking office, a small gift shop and toilets. The trams usually operate a 20 minute service when running. Wheelchair passengers will have to be lifted onto the cars. There used to be an overhead wire over the track and the car had trolley poles. This was for signalling from the driver to the engineer at Halfway. Each section has its own engineer. Portable radios are now used for this purpose. The wire and poles are being removed.

At Victoria Station it is a single line. In the middle there is a conduit 14" deep in which the cable goes. The tramcar has a cable attached to it to pull the car up and this is connected to the winding drum at Halfway. The tram proceeds at 5 M.P.H with a maximum speed of 6½ M.P.H. up a narrow section of old road. Traffic is not allowed on this section when the trams are running. Reaching Black Gate crossing the traffic light will automatically change in front of the tram.

You will notice the driver radioing the engineer telling him that he is approaching the lights and notifying him when they have changed. The traffic lights controlling the tram movement are the correct tramway type.

Just after passing Black Gate Crossing you will meet the other tram coming down. You will notice that there is a point in the line and the track you take will depend on which tram you are in, as each tram keeps to its own line from here, otherwise the rope would get crossed. The trams on the lower section are numbed 4 St Tudno and 5 St Silio, number 4 tram keeps to the left-hand track. The track now widens for the two trams to pass.

Your tram may slow down or even stop. This is because the tram going down hill is approaching the traffic lights and has to wait for them to change. Your car will then proceed. The track looks as though there are three rails from here to Halfway. The tram operating on the left uses the left outer rail and the centre rail. The right hand tram uses the outer right rail and the centre rail. Also there are the two grooves in the centre of each track to take the ropes.

The two intermediate stops at Black Gate and Beaver Lodge, at the end of Tyn y Coed Road, are not now used.

HALFWAY
(489 feet)

Arriving at Halfway you will be required to alight and walk a short distance past the winding houses and sheds to board the tramcar for the top section. The top section is operated by rope too, but on a different method. Each of the cars is connected to rope from the winding house. There is also a rope from each car that goes up to the summit station round a pulley and returns down the line to the other car. Thus the cars help to balance each over. The ropes are offset from centre. The drivers on this section are also in radio contact with their own engineer at Halfway.

When the car departs it moves up single track until it reaches the passing loop. As the car ascends notice the Great Orme Mine on your left and watch out for the ungated road crossing. The cars on this upper section are numbered 6 St Seiriol and 7 St Trillo, number 7 keeping to the lefthand track in the passing loop. The driver will check the indicator on the point to make sure his car number is showing. The car will then take the appropriate line. After passing the down car the car will enter the top single line section setting the upper point as it passes over it which resets the indicator. The car going down will also have reset the lower point as it passes over it. The track is now single line to the summit.

SUMMIT
(637 feet)

The tramcar you are on may enter the Summit Station so that you can dismount under cover. The station was rebuilt in 1992

126

including a small visitors centre and toilets. On the right of the tram station a short walk will bring you the summit complex which has a cafe. The summit of the Great Orme is 679 feet above sea level. You are on the highest piece of land jutting out to sea on the British coast. On a clear day there are excellent views both over Llandudno Bay, Conwy Bay, Anglesey and Liverpool Bay. You may be lucky and be able to see Ireland, the Isle of Man and the mountains of the Lake District. In summer you may want to descend the Great Orme to Happy Valley using the cable car.

How to Get There

Coming by road enter Llandudno by the A470, follow this road past the supermarket, and go straight on at

A familiar sight at Llandudno — the Great Orme Tramway. No 4 St Tudno is standing at the Halfway station.

the roundabout. You are now in Mostyn Street. Continue straight up Mostyn Street and you will come to Upper Mostyn Street. At the end turn left into Church Walks. Victoria Station is on your right. You may find parking difficult in the season.

Most of the local bus services running in Llandudno terminate in Gloddaeth Street. Should you get off here walk to the roundabout and turn left into Upper Mostyn Street. Walk to the end at the junction, turn left into Church walks, Victoria Station is along this road on your right

To get to Victoria Station in Church Walk, from the Llandudno railway station turn left outside Llandudno railway station into Augusta Street, carry on into Madoc Street. At the end of Madoc Street, cross over Lloyd Street and take the street which is just offset to the right, Chapel Street. Passing the Tourist Information Centre on your left, continue to the end and go straight across Gloddaeth Street to Arvon Avenue.

At the end of the Avenue you will come to a multiple road junction.

Bear to the right and turn into Old Road. There is a sign for the Tramway on the corner. In 1997 this was the only sign for the tramway in Llandudno. Old Road leads to Church Walks and Victoria Station is opposite you on the left.

Alternatively from the station walk down the road opposite Vaughan Street to the roundabout. Turn left into Mostyn Street, the main shopping street in Llandudno, then follow the instructions for arriving by car from Mostyn Street.

Opening Times & Details
They operate from Easter to the end of October.

Details from: Conwy County Borough Council, Contracts Department, Tramway Operations Manger, Maesdu Depot, Llandudno. Conwy C.B. LL30 1HF.

4
MINIATURE LINES

CONWY VALLEY RAILWAY MUSEUM

The Railway Museum is situated in the old goods yard at Betws-y-Coed opposite the station. In the 1960s the passing loop, down platform and goods yard sidings were removed, except for the line on which the standard gauge rolling stock now stands. In 1973 the site was obtained from British Railways. The Museum and Miniature Railway were started in 1977. It is operated as a private venture, the present owner obtaining the museum in 1985.

The Museum has a Gift and Model Shop in which you will find toy and model trains of various gauges, including N gauge, OO gauge and G gauge.

There is a cafe on site, which is housed in an old MK1 B.R. Coach. Wheelchairs cannot get into the cafe but on a fine day it is pleasant to sit at the tables which are outside the cafe. There are toilets in the cafe for customers.

Originally the station at Betws-y-Coed had a goods wharf known as Cei Llechi (Slate Quay). This was to take the slate from an area including Dolwyddelan and Cwm Penmachno. The slate wharf is still on the site though the 7¼" railway has breached it. To see its full length you will need to take a tram ride. Alongside part of the wharf is a line on which there are various items of standard gauge rolling stock:

Southern Railway 1935 parcel van.

Pullman coach, still on its American bogies, which British Railways converted into a camping coach.

A General Utility Van built in 1950 by B.R. at York to L.N.E.R patterns; this van was used for carrying cars so that they would be under cover.

An old guards van built in Swindon in 1895 for branch line use and converted for the use of fitters in the 1943.

A Southern Railway parcel guards van built at Ashford in 1935. This now houses the museum's L.G.B. layout.

The cafe kitchen is in a L.M.S. parcel guards van built at Wolverhampton in 1939. This is a 6 wheeled vehicle.

The tiny locomotive Sian takes passengers along the 7½" miniature railway at Conwy Valley Railway Museum, Betws-y-Coed. 153330 arrives with the 14.03 for Bleanau Ffestiniog.

The cafe an ex-B.R. Mk1 TSO was built in 1954 at Eastleigh for use on the Southern Region of British Rail. You will notice when you enter it that 16 seats have been removed and replaced by the counter.

Some of the stock is in the private section of the grounds but can be viewed from the train or tram.

On site for the children under 10 years are small cars, and a drive it yourself tram engine on a 7¼" gauge line.

In the grounds there is a 7¼" miniature railway. This line originally only operated as an out and back service from the museum to the south end of the site. The present owner has extended the line so that the circuit is now a flattened figure eight. The ride on this railway will take you under the footbridge. This is the only one in the country that has three gauges running under it, the 7¼" gauge railway, the 15" gauge tramway, and the standard gauge line and platform. You go past the standard gauge rolling stock and round the south curve until you are once more facing north. As you pass the sheds you will see a gallows turntable.

The line then passes the cafe- and runs alongside the car park. At the north end you may see squirrels and rabbits if the weather is right. Going round the north curve you return on a bridge over a small pond in which there are fishes. You will now return to the south curve. Then heading north you will run parallel to the branch line all the way to the north curve. Round the curve and back to the station. This run covers about 1¼ miles and takes about 8 minutes.

Automatic colour light signalling is being installed on the railway. Operating on the railway are various types of motive power. There are 3 coal fired steam locomotives, one diesel outline locomotive with a petrol engine, and a battery electric

A busy day at the Conwy Valley Railway Museum. The 15" tram on the left with Sian and the diesel on the loop line. Old Rube pulls away with passengers.

Crocodile. Sometimes there are visiting locomotives.

Also on site there is a 15" gauge electric tram, which runs from one end of the site to the other alongside the standard gauge railway. The tram was specially made for the site in Walsall. Work started in 1988 and it was brought to the museum in 1989. In 1990 it ran from the museum to the north end of the site. The line was extended to the footbridge for the 1996 season. At the end of the summer season it was further extended, so that by March 1997 the track had been laid all the way to the southern boundary of the site. The total ride you get on the tram is just over ½ a mile. The tram operates on 110 volts D.C.

In the museum there are dioramas, built by the late Jack Nelson, and model railway layouts, which you can start at the press of a button; also a 15" gauge ¼ scale model of British Railways 70000 Britannia, which it is hoped to run in the museum grounds some time in the future. There are also extensive displays of railway memorabilia.

How to Get There

Coming by train to get to the site cross over the footbridge. Should you be in a wheelchair then you will have to go round by road. Go out of the station and turn left, at the main road turn left. When you come to Ffordd Hen Eglwys/Old Church, follow it until you come to the museum.

Coming by road.

From the Bangor direction on the A5 continue through the village until you pass the road to the station. Ffordd Hen Eglwys/Old Church Road is the next on the left.

From Llandudno follow the A470 until it meets the A5, turn right over the Waterloo Bridge.*

From Blaenau Ffestiniog follow the A470 until it meet the A5, turn left and follow it over the Waterloo Bridge.*

From the south on the A5. This road will lead you over the Waterloo Bridge.*

*After crossing the Waterloo Bridge go past the two petrol stations and take first right into Ffordd Hen Eglwys/Old Church Road. Continue along this road until you come to the museum car park. The gate to the car park is locked at night when the museum is closed.

Opening Times & Details

The museum is open every day from Easter to the end of October and weekends during the winter.

Details from: Conwy Valley Railway Museum, The Old Goods Yard, Betws-y-Coed, Conwy C.B. LL24 0AL.

FAIRBOURNE & BARMOUTH STEAM RAILWAY

The original line at Fairbourne was laid to convey building materials in 1895. It was constructed by Mr A McDougall whose name is associated with flour. It was worked with horses and the gauge was 2 feet. In 1916 it was converted to 15" gauge and steam locomotives were employed. It followed the original line for most of the way with a few small diversions.

The original line finished at Porth Penrhyn but over the years it has been extended to Pont Penrhyn. It was closed in 1940 to reopen part way in 1947 and all the way to the ferry for the 1948 season. The length of the line is about 1¾ miles. By 1983 the railway was run down and in 1984 Mr J Ellerton purchased the railway. The new company converted it to 12¼" gauge, completing by 1986.

New locomotives were introduced which are half scale replicas of famous narrow gauge locomotives.

No1 Lynton and Barnstaple tank

No 2 N.W.N.G.R. tank Beddgelert.

No 4 Darjeeling and Himalayas tender engine.

No 5 Leek and Manifold tank.

A diesel based on a General Motors type. Today the railway still has both coal-fired steam engines and diesel locomotives.

In 1997 the present owners purchased the railway. The locomotives may be facing in either direction, as there is a circular loop at the far end and a turntable at Fairbourne. The coaches are enclosed and you can travel first class for an extra charge. Some of the carriages have only got doors on one side. The locomotive and carriage sheds are at Fairbourne. The main station has a booking office and shop. Also on the platform there is a cafe.

The single journey takes about 20 minutes and the round trip

The Yeo, one of the locomotives on the Fairbourne and Barmouth miniature railway.

1 hour. On leaving Fairbourne the train travels towards the sea alongside Beach Road. You will notice that the train travels over road crossings and has priority. When the original railway was built it was on private estate and did not require a Light Railway Order or Parliamentary sanction to cross the road. During the time the railway has been in existence the council have taken over the roads. The railway still owns the land six feet either side of the line. This creates a legal anathema. At the crossing points the county road has a right of way but the train has priority. On reaching the end of Beach Road the train takes a right-handed curve to get on to the seaside of Penrhyn Road North and heads towards Barmouth.

The train will now follow the road until you come to the station that used to be called Golf House. The 1984 owners decided to rename the station to give it the longest station name in Wales. GORSAFAWDDACHADRAIGDDANHEDDOGLEDDOLON-PENRHYNAREUDRAETHCEREDIGION. This loosely means The Mawddach station with its Dragon's teeth on the North Penrhyn Drive by the golden sands of Cardigan Bay. Dragon's teeth were the local name given to the tank traps, which were put on the beach during the last war.

The train continues to the passing point at Pont Penrhyn. The drivers will exchange tokens here. Also notice that the track is laid on a continuous concrete slab. From here the railway continues and you will eventually pass through a tunnel. This was built to try and keep the line clear from blowing sand. Should you be on the first train after a night that has had a bad storm, the train may have to stop while the driver clears the line of sand. You will then come into the circular loop. Normally the train takes the west left hand line to Porth Penrhyn station. The station is built on a curve.

At the station the locomotive will run round the train and you will return the way you came. However when specials are run they may go through the station and return on the east side of the circle. At the station there is the Pullman Pavilion Restaurant and toilets. There are good views across the estuary. A passenger ferry service operates from near the station to Barmouth harbour when the state of the tide is right. You can also catch the ferry from Barmouth to the railway.

How to Get There

If you come by train, when you get off walk towards the level crossing and you will see the station on the opposite of the road.

Fairbourne village is off the A493 Dolgellau to Tywyn coast road, you will see the village clearly signposted. Drive down this road towards the village. After going over the level crossing you will see the station on your left. To park turn first right after coming over the crossing and there is car parking on your right.

Opening Times & Details

The railway operates from Easter to the end of October. There is a limited service at the start and end of the season.

Details from: The Fairbourne Railway, Beach Road, Fairbourne. Dolgellau. Gwynedd. LL38 2PZ.

JOYS OF LIFE COUNTRY PARK BETHESDA

The Joys of Life Country Park is a private garden and nature reserve. It is on the B4409 at Bethesda. The park is 12 acres. Part of the area is kept as a nature reserve, with a lake. You can walk right round the lake and there is a bird hide from which you can watch any visiting birds and look round the area. There are toilets on site and a picnic area. There is no cafe on site so you are encouraged to bring your own picnic and sit at the tables provided.

There is a 5" gauge miniature railway at ground level. This is The Little Edwardian Children's Railway. The railway is a 1/5 scale model based on a North Wales quarry railway at the turn of the century. The

This quaint 5" miniature railway runs through the Joys of Life Country Park at Bethesda. Entering the passing loop, Faith arrives at Moles Hill station.

135

owner has made most of the railway. It consists of a main station with a single line running through a deep cutting and across a level crossing to the next station. This station has a passing loop. From here the line enters a short tunnel and continues to a circle loop at the end. The train will then return along the same line to the main station. Semaphore signals have been installed all along the line with signal boxes to control them. The signal boxes have interlocking lever frames similar to the type used at the turn of the century.

A coal fired steam locomotive is normally run. There is also a petrol driven and a battery electric locomotive. The rolling stock has wagons with seats for the children to ride on. There are also various items of goods stock that can be attached to the train.

How to Get There

The nearest main road is the A5, coming from the Betws-y-Coed direction, just as you pass the sign for Bethesda you will come to the B4409 for Tregarth, turn left into it. From the A55 and Bangor direction travel through Bethesda. Just as you are leaving the village you will see the sign for the B4409 for Tregarth, turn right into it. Follow the B4409 for about ¾ mile. The entrance is on the right hand side of the road. There is a car park on the site.

Opening Times & Details

The site is open during school holidays at Easter week, early May Bank Holiday weekend, and late May Spring Bank Holiday Week. Then from the middle of July to the first week in September it is open Monday to Friday. Also open on August Bank Holiday weekend.

The owners Mr and Mrs Robinson provide Bed and Breakfast in the house. So if you want to talk about the railway why not stay there for a night or more.

Details from: Joys of Life Country Park, Coed y Parc, Bethesda, Gwynedd. LL57 4YW.

RHYL MINIATURE RAILWAY

The railway is situated round the Marine Lake. The railway is 15" gauge and operates in the high season. It operates both steam and diesel locomotives. The main station for the railway is alongside the A548. During the winter and spring of 1998 Welsh Water are installing a new storm tank system at the side of the lake. This has necessitated taking up some of the track. The railway has been told that it should all be reinstated by summer 1998. When this work has been competed the railway should be in fine working order with a new station and most of the track relayed.

How to Get There

It is on the A548, as you enter Rhyl from the Abergele direction you will cross a bridge. Carry straight on keeping the fun fair on your left, the Marine Lake is on the right hand side.

From Prestatyn and Rhuddlan follow the A548 towards Abergele and Colwyn Bay. After coming out of the one way system you will come into Wellington Road, the Marine Lake on your left.

Coming by train, when you leave the station go straight forward down Bodfor Street to Kinmel Street. Turn left and walk to the end of the road, turn right into Elwy Street and then left onto Wellington Road, this is the A548. The Marine Lake will be on your left hand side, it is ¾ mile from the station. Should you want to take a bus then the Bus Station is on your right as you leave the Railway Station.

Opening Times & Details

The railway is open Sunday and Monday at Easter, May Bank Holiday and Whitsuntide. Then most Sundays till mid September. During the school summer holiday it is open every day except Saturday.

Details from: Rhyl Marina Lake Railway, Wellington Road, Rhyl, Denbighshire. LL18 1LN.

5
OTHER ATTRACTIONS

ANGLESEY MODEL VILLAGE

The Model Village and gardens are the work of the owner. He has created the models to 1/12th scale. The models are based on buildings on Anglesey, and need to be seen to appreciate the details. The gardens in the village are well laid out and gardeners will find the variety of plants interesting.

There is a model railway, which has also been built to 1/12th scale. The gauge is 4⅜" and is double track, It operates in the centre of the model village. The locomotives are powered by battery. The line has a station and crosses a small pond by a bridge. The train will pull away from the station and complete one circuit of the line. It will then wait in the station until the battery has been recharged before continuing on another circuit.

All parts of the village are accessible by wheelchair. In the village there is a toilet which will take a wheelchair. There is also a tearoom serving light refreshments. A small picnic and children's play area, including a children's self drive locomotive.

How to Get There

The Model Village is situated on the A4080 road.

Enter Ynys M n (Anglesey) on the A5, crossing the Menai Straits on the Britannia Bridge. Take the first exit left, and turn left on to the A4080 heading to Llanfairpwllgwyngyll. As you leave the slip road you enter Llanfairpwllgwyngyll, this is the old A5 road. About ½ mile on the A4080 takes the left-hand road at the junction for Newborough. Follow the A4080 passing through Brynsiencyn. At Dwyran the road takes a sharp left turn. The model village is about ½ mile on the left.

There is a free Coach and Car Park.

Opening Times & Details

The Model Village is open from Easter to the end of October.

Details from: The Anglesey Model Village, Parc, Newborough, Ynys M n, LL61 6RS.

CORRIS RAILWAY MUSEUM

The Corris Railway started in 1859 as a tramroad worked by horses. It was called The Corris, Machynlleth and River Dovey Tramroad. The purpose was to take the slate from the quarries in the Dulas valley above Corris down the quays on the Afon Dovey, west of Machynlleth at Derwenlas and Morben. The line was gravity worked for part of the way. The slate would be put into small ships to be taken to Aberdyfi (Aberdovey) for transhipment to larger vessels

In 1863 the main line railway from Newtown to Aberystwyth reached Machynlleth. The Corris had to abandon the lines west of Machynlleth. A new goods yard with transhipment facilities was built at Machynlleth and the Tramroad changed its name to the Corris Railway. The gauge of the line is 2'-3", the same as the Talyllyn Railway. The Corris Railway started to carry passengers in the early 1870s. In 1878 steam locomotives and passenger coaches were ordered. In the early 1900s the slate traffic started to decline and a proposal was made to build an electric line from upper Corris to meet with the Talyllyn at Abergynolwyn. Nothing came of the idea, but buses were introduced to replace the horse drawn vehicles that had been on this route.

In 1930 the company was sold to the Great Western Railway and passenger traffic ceased. Due to the state of the bridge across the Afon Dyfi the line was closed in 1948 and the railway was dismantled within a year.

The railway has constructed a new station in the yard near to the health centre. The line has been laid down to the shed at Moraespoeth. This is alongside the main road but please do not park here as the main road is narrow and there is only room for staff parking. The railway is going to make a station alongside the shed so trains will run from Corris and passengers can visit the shed. It is hoped to have the railway running to here in Easter 1999. The railway has permission to extend beyond for just over 2 miles. The next object is to get to Tyn-y-Coed car park and picnic site.

Two of the engines and some of the rolling stock are still in use on the Talyllyn Railway. Should you travel the road from Corris down to Machynlleth you will still see parts of the old track bed. The road has been widened in places and has encroached on the track bed. The bridge footings across the river Dovey are still visible. Even some of the old station buildings are still in use as bus shelters.

The museum has a shop with selection of books and serves light refreshments. Inside there are displays of the history of the line and part of one of the old coaches.

How to Get There

The Museum is in the village of Corris just off the A487. Turn off the main road by the Braichgoch Hotel, towards Corris. The turn coming from the north makes a hairpin bend and is not recommended. Carry on down this road until you pass the toilets then turn right into the museum yard. There is only a small car parking area here. The Tourist Information Centre (summer only) is in the Corris Craft Centre, this is the best place to park. This is north of Corris on the A487. Park at the south end of the car park. From the car park make your way to the old road that is at the back of the site. Turn left on to it and walk all the way to the end. When you come to the main road, cross over and on the other side to the left is a footpath. The path has only one small step but is very steep, there are small seats on each corner for you to rest on. It zigzags down to the village and comes out opposite the museum yard. The Tourist Information Centre is in the Craft Centre complex. The nearest railway station is Machynlleth and bus services No 2, 30, & 34 operate to the end of the road.

Opening Times & Details

The Museum is run entirely by volunteers and is open from the end of May to the end of October. In early and late season the Museum is closed on Saturdays. However due to relying on volunteers it may be shut at other times.

Details from: Mr P Guest, 38 Underwood Close, Callow Hill, Redditch, Worcestershire. B97 5YZ.

INTERNATIONAL MODEL RAILWAY WORLD LLANGOLLEN

The exhibition is at The Lower Dee Exhibition Centre, in the same building as the Dr Who Experience. It is situated in part of the Dapol factory complex. There are exhibits on several floors showing over 60 years of model railways from various manufactures. All gauges of model railway are shown and many of the layouts can be operated. There is also an exhibit that features live steam locomotives, which run subject to availability. You can tour the factory, when it is in production, and see models being made. Conducted tours are also available round the factory. Unfortunately you will have to climb the stairs to visit the different floors. There is a shop and cafe.

How to Get There
The exhibition is in Mill Street, which is the A539 Wrexham road. The car park and a public car park is on the right from Llangollen. From the station walk up to the bridge, and cross over the road. You can walk along the main road, or on a footpath along the Dee, which is the site of the old railway line. There is a proposal to develop a single track railway from the station to a halt by the exhibition.

Opening Times & Details
The exhibition is open all the year round except Christmas Day, Boxing Day and New Year's Day. Details from: Dapol, Lower Dee Exhibition Centre, Mill Street, Llangollen, Denbighshire. LL20 8RX.

KIVOLI CENTRE BALA
The Kivoli Centre is on the site of the old Bala Town station. It has a large stock of both British and Continental model railway equipment. The range covers from N gauge to HO gauge including Hoe & Hom, and 0 gauge kits.

There are also model railway displays and layouts that you can visit which are being improved as time permits. These should give you a good idea on how the different types of models can be used together. You will find the owner most helpful. Should you have some time to spare the centre is well worth a visit.

How to Get There
From the Corwen direction on the A494 as you enter Bala cross the bridge and turn left into the B4391 (Llangynog).

From Dolgellau travel through Bala and turn right into the B4391 (Llangynog).

From Trawsfynydd on the A4212 you will come to the main A494 road in Bala, the B4391 (Llangynog) is in front of you slightly to the right.

Follow the B4391 and take the second turning on the left into the

Industrial Estate and take first left. The Kivoli Centre is on your right. There is only a small car park. Should you want to stay in Bala the main car park and toilets are the first turning on the left on the B4391, and only a short walk away.

Opening Times & Details
The Centre is open Monday to Friday all summer, but may be shut some days in winter.
Details from: Kivoli Centre, 1 Station Yard, Bala. Gwynedd. LL23 7NL.

LEIN AMLWCH RAILWAY CENTRE
(Lein, line. Amlwch, land bordering a lake)
The Lein Amlwch Railway Centre is housed in the old goods shed, which belonged to Amlwch Station. The Anglesey Central Railway built the line from the junction with the main Bangor to Holyhead line at Caerwen. The line was open to Amlwch in 1866 for goods and 1897 for passenger traffic. The length of the line was 17½ miles. Amlwch is the most northerly town in Wales, making the end of the line the furthest north in Wales. The line closed for passenger traffic in 1964. A new section of track was laid through Amlwch from near the station throat to the Industrial Estate. Railtrack owns the line for 17.37 miles from Caerwen with Associated Octel owning the rest of the line as a private siding. The traffic to the Octel plant ended in 1995.

The Isle of Anglesey Railways Limited are hoping to reopen the line and run train services once more. The goods shed in which the centre is housed was built in 1895. Just before you enter the centre note, on the left, part of the edge of the original platform at the station. The centre contains a shop selling model railway equipment including N gauge and OO gauge, railway books and videos etc. Upstairs there are several model railways in N gauge and OO gauge. An EM gauge model of Amlwch station as it existed in passenger days is in the process of construction. There is also a display showing the history of the line.

Though there is no cafe at the centre there is one next door.

How to Get There
To get to the centre from Bangor direction after coming over Britannia Bridge, take the second turning off the A5, the A5025 Amlwch. Follow this road into Amlwch, after going over the railway crossing the centre

is on your left. There is a small car park at the centre. Should this be full you could turn right after crossing the railway following the road to the main street. Turn right across the railway once more and turn right alongside the line. This leads into a car park. From the far end there is a footpath to the A5025. Turn right, cross the railway and the centre is on the left.

Opening Times & Details

The centre is open all year, April to August every day. September to March Friday to Monday.

Details from: Lein Amlwch Railway Centre, Amlwch, Ynys Mon, LL68 9TG.

LLECHWEDD SLATE CAVERNS
BLAENAU FFESTINIOG

Slate was first discovered in the Blaenau Ffestiniog area in 1755. Quarries were opened up, and packhorse or cart transported the slate through Llan Ffestiniog down to Maentwrog. From here it was taken down to wharves on the Dwyryd and put in shallow boats to be taken down river to be transferred to the large sailing ships. With the coming of the railways from 1836 the quarries started to send the slate by rail.

John Greaves had come to North Wales in 1830. Slate was first found at Llechwedd (slope of the hill) after 3 years hard work in 1849. As the quarry developed tunnels were dug into the hillside to get at the slate. The slate on the site was mined more then quarried. From the first tunnel dug the levels were then numbered upward 1-7 and downward A-I, 16 floors altogether covering over a 1000-ft vertical distance.

As the slate was taken out it left large caverns in the ground, and large tips above ground. Only about 10% of the rock and slate removed will become a finished product. With the decline in the demand for slate, quarries were closed. Llechwedd was opened up as a tourist attraction in 1972.

MINER'S TRAMWAY

The Miner's Tramway was the first part of the tourist attraction. The line is to 1'-11½" gauge but is due to be regauged to 2'-0". The line is over 1000 feet long. It travels into the mountain on the level. Very shortly it comes out into daylight, you may be

This tramway takes you into the mountain at Llechwedd Slate Caverns where miners used to labour in Blaenau Ffestiniog.

able to see the present quarry at work.

You will then continue into another tunnel to the end of the line. The trains are controlled by colour light signals and there is a passing loop part way into the tunnel. At the end of the line you will leave the train for a short walk and a talk by a guide. Remounting your train you then travel a short way back to another cavern where the guide explains how the slate was removed. Remounting a train you will then be brought back to the slate splitting shed were you will be shown how slate is split and dressed.

Battery electric locomotives provide the traction. There are four locomotives working on this level and two working in another part of the quarry in which slate is still being produced. When the quarry opened to the public in 1972 three locomotives were obtained. Two of the locomotives had been used under Bristol on a sewerage system and then in tunnels under the Pennines. The other one had been used on reservoir schemes in Scotland, tunnels in Askham and worked in tin mines in Cornwall. All three were refurbished at Boston Lodge. The quarry had used battery electric locomotives before this and one is on display in the museum section. The passenger wagons are converted contractor jubilee skips. These were stripped down and rebuilt to carry four passengers each.

DEEP MINE

On the site there is also the Deep Mine, which has a special constructed 24 seat car. The gauge is 3'-0" and the incline gradient of 1:1.8. This was opened in 1979 but was improved by extra effects in 1992.You enter the car on Floor 2 which is 849ft above sea level and descend to Floor A 99ft lower. You will then walk through the tunnels and caverns being guided by a light and sound system. You are required to wear hard hats for safety, as some of the roofs are low, so if you are tall you will have to duck or grouse. The walk will take you down 61 steps to a lower floor

An old wagon amid the bleak terrain at Llechwedd Slate Caverns.

32ft below. When you walk down these modern steps just think about the miners climbing up on ladders. During the tour you will also pass an underground lake. As you rejoin the car on Floor B you will be 450ft beneath the mountaintop. The car will then take you to the surface. Should you be unable to walk down the steps or are claustrophobic this part of the mine is not recommended.

On the site there is a shop and a cafeteria, which are open all the year. You can walk round the Victorian Village with shops and pub but they are only open in the season. There is a small museum giving details of the history of the quarry and the surrounding district. Outside there is a display of various types of trucks used by the mines. You can see the original incline where the slate was taken down to both the Ffestiniog Railway and the L.N.W.R. This passes under the turnpike road now A470. The incline was twin tracked starting on Floor 3. It was gravity worked, the full wagons pulling up the empty ones. Last used in 1964 the track on the incline was removed in 1972 to be used on the miner's tramway. Electricity was used in the mine from 1890 and a steam locomotive was converted to electric in 1927 supplied from an overhead wire at 220V D.C.

Each tour will take about 30 minutes, but at peak times you may have to queue before you get on. In winter each tour is operated one after the other so you can cover both without waiting. On some weeks during the winter each will be shut down for a short period for maintenance.

How to Get There

The site entrance is off the A470. Coming from Betws-y-Coed direction it is the first entrance on your left after you enter Blaenau Ffestiniog.

From the town centre take the A470 north from the town, as the road starts to climb you will come to the entrance on your right.

Should you come by train it is advisable to get a bus from the Queens Hotel. The bus stop is in the car park at the side of the hotel by the door to the Ffestiniog Railway shop. You can walk after leaving the station turn left and follow the A470. This is not recommended, as the road becomes narrow with no footpath and high walls. It is proposed to improve this road in the future.

Opening Times & Details

The caverns are open every day from 10.00 except Christmas Day, Boxing Day and New Year's Day. The last tours are March to September 17.15. October to February 16.15

Details from: Llechwedd Slate Caverns, Blaenau Ffestiniog. Gwynedd. LL41 3NB.

LLYWERNOG MINE MUSEUM

Mining activity on the site can be traced from 1745. There is a guided deep main tour and it is possible to visit a prospecting tunnel dating from 1790s. Over the life of the mine both silver and lead were extracted. The museum was started in 1973 and more attractions are being added as time permits. There is a tea-room with gift shop.

There is a short length of 22" gauge track on which there is a tub. The narrow gauge railway of 2'-0" gauge is partly dual gauged with a 1'-8" line. This line is used as a demonstration. It is proposed to upgrade the 2'-0" gauge line to passenger carrying use in the future. Battery electric and diesel powered locomotives are to be seen. Three of the battery locomotives are named Anode, Cathode, and Diode.

The museum houses a small collection of Hornby Dublo 3-rail track, Hornby O gauge 2-rail tin plate, and some Meccano Models.

How to Get There

The Museum is situated on the north side of the A44, 1 mile on the Aberystwyth side of Ponterwyd. There is a large coach and car park

Opening Times & Details

The museum is open from Mid March to the end of October, and in November and December on Tuesday to Thursday.

Details from: Llywernog Mine Museum, Ponterwyd. Ceredigion. SY23 3AB.

MOSTYNS CAFE LLANDUDNO

Mostyns cafe bar is at 66 Mostyn Street Llandudno.

The G scale railway was installed in May 1997. The track runs at picture rail height between the two front rooms. Normally there is a tram and trailer car running round. The cafe has both L.G.B. and Bachmann stock. You can tell your friends that you sat in a cafe in Mostyn Street and watched a tram go by.

How to Get There

From the station walk down the road opposite Vaughan Street to the roundabout. Turn left into Mostyn Street, the main shopping street in Llandudno*.

G gauge trams on the track running at picture rail height at Mostyns Cafe, Llandudno.

Coming by road enter Llandudno by the A470, follow this road past the supermarket. And go straight on at the roundabout. You are now in Mostyn Street *.

*Continue up Mostyn street till you come to Lloyd street on the left with the National Westminster Bank on the corner. Walk past the bank, go past Plumes and next door is the entrance to the cafe. Go up the stairs to the first floor.

Most of the local bus services running in Llandudno operate down Mostyn Street or terminate in Gloddaeth Street. Should you get off here walk to the roundabout and turn right into Mostyn Street. Cross Market Street and the cafe will be on your left near the end of the block.

Opening Times & Details
The cafe is open all the year round. Snacks and main meals are available all day.

Details from: Mostyns Cafe Bar 66 Mostyn Street Llandudno. Conwy C.B. LL30 2SB.

PENRHYN CASTLE INDUSTRIAL RAILWAY MUSEUM
AMGUEDDFA RHEILFFORDD DIWYDIANNOL
CASTELL PENRHYN

The industrial railway museum is in Penrhyn Castle, which is owned by The National Trust. It is situated at Llandegai outside Bangor. It is the only museum in Britain dedicated to industrial railway locomotives and rolling stock. There are industrial locomotives from various works and quarries. Charles is one of the locomotives that were used on the quarry line from Bethesda to

Port Penrhyn. You can see Fire Queen and other vehicles used on the Padarn line which operated from the Dinorwic quarry to Port Dinorwic. There is a display of 2 feet gauge locomotives in the museum, and outside a display of track and wagons. The museum has a cafe and toilets for gentlemen, ladies and disabled.

How to Get There
The entrance to the Castle grounds is off the A5122. From the junction of the A55 and A5, take the A5122 for Bangor. The entrance is 1 mile on the right. From Bangor take the A5122 towards Conwy the entrance is 2 miles from the town centre on the left. The Castle is 1 mile along the drive from the entrance.

Opening Times & Details
The museum is open daily, except Tuesdays from the end of March to the end of October. Details from: Penrhyn Castle, Near Bangor. Gwynedd. LL57 4HN.

KEY TO DRAWINGS
Standard Gauge Lines & Stations Open

Standard Gauge Lines with No Service

Standard Gauge Lines & Stations Closed

Narrow Gauge Lines & Main Stations

Cable Hauled Lines

Other Railway Attractions

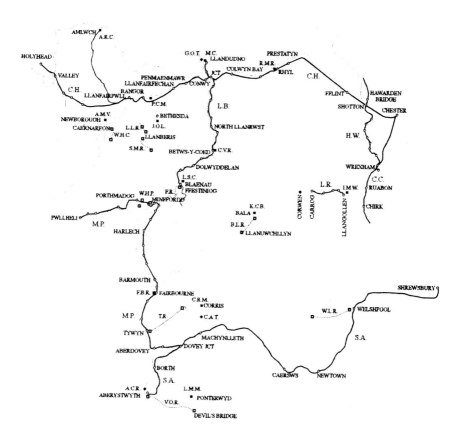

INDEX

151

APOLOGY

Due to a printer's error this section has been manually incorporated.

STATION NAMES AND OTHER ATTRACTIONS

Standard Gauge & Narrow Gauge Railway Lines

BALA LAKE RAILWAY	B.L.R.
FFESTINIOG RAILWAY	F.R.
GREAT ORME TRAMWAY	G.O.T.
LLANBERIS LAKE RAILWAY	L.L.R.
SNOWDON MOUNTAIN RAILWAY	S.M.R.
TALYLLYN RAILWAY	T.R.
VALE OF RHEIDOL RAILWAY	V.O.R.
WELSH HIGHLAND CAERNARFON	W.H.C.
WELSH HIGHLAND PORTHMADOG	W.H.P.
WELSHPOOL & LLANFAIR RAILWAY	W.L.R.
CHESTER — CHIRK	C.C.
CHESTER — HOLYHEAD	C.H.
HAWARDEN BRIDGE — WREXHAM CENTRAL	H.W.
LLANDUDNO — BLAENAU FFESTINIOG	L.B.
LLANGOLLEN RAILWAY	L.R.
MACHYNLLETH — PWLLHELI	M.P.
SHREWSBURY — ABERYSTWYTH	S.A.

Map Number is for Ordnance Survey Landranger 1:50 000 scale

STATION NAME	LINE	MAP No	Reference
ABERDOVEY	M.P.	135	SN 606960
ABERERCH	M.P.	123	SH 403360
ABERGELE & PENSARN	C.H.	116	SH 946787
ABERGYNOLWYN	T.R.	124	SH 670064
ABERFFRWD	V.O.R.	135	SN 687787
ABERYSTWYTH	S.A.& V.O.R.	135	SN 585815
BANGOR	C.H.	114&115	SH 575716
BARMOUTH	M.P.	124	SH 611158
BERWYN	L.R.	125	SJ 198431
BETWS Y COED	L.B.	115	SH 795565
BLAENAU FFESTINIOG	F.R. L.B.	115	SH 700459
BODORGAN	C.H.	114	SH 386702
BORTH	S.A.	135	SN 609901
BOSTON LODGE	F.R.	124	SH 585379
BRYN HYNOD HALT	B.L.R.	125	SH 911350
BRYNGLAS	T.R.	135	SH 628031
BUCKLEY	H.W.	117	SJ 295633
CAERGWRLE	H.W.	117	SJ 309572
CAERNARFON	W.H.C.	114&115	SH 479625
CAERSWS	S.A.	136	SO 028919
CAPEL BANGOR	V.O.R.	135	SN 647798
CARROG	L.R.	125	SJ 118435
CASTLE CAEREINION	W.L.R.	125	SJ 161059

STATION NAME	LINE	MAP No	Reference
CEFN Y BEDD	H.W.	17	SJ 310562
CEI LLYDAN	L.L.R.	115	SH 574614
CHIRK	C.C.	126	SJ 284379
COLWYN BAY	C.H.	116	SH 851793
CONWY	C.H.	115	SH 781774
CRICCIETH	M.P.	123	SH 497380
CYFRONYDD	W.L.R.	125	SJ 138077
CYNFAL	T.R.	135	SH 611020
DDUALLT	F.R.	124	SH 678421
DEESIDE HALT	L.R.	125	SJ 172424
DEGANWY	L.B.	115	SH 779791
DEVIL'S BRIDGE	V.O.R.	135	SN 738769
DINAS	W.H.C.	115	SH 476586
DOLARDDYN CROSSING	W.L.R.	125	SJ 152063
DOLGAROG	L.B.	115	SH 783670
DOLGOCH	T.R.	135	SH 652045
DOLWYDDELAN	L.B.	115	SH 738531
DOVEY JUNCTION	S.A.	135	SN 696980
DYFFRYN ARDUDWY	M.P.	124	SH 581233
FACH GOCH	T.R.	135	SH 605016
FAIRBOURNE	M.P.	124	SH 616129
FFLINT	C.H.	117	SJ 245731
GILFACH DDU	L.L.R.	115	SH 585604
GLAN CONWY	L.B.	116	SH 802760
GLANRAFON	V.O.R.	135	SN 615804
GLOGWYN	S.M.R.	115	SH 607561
GLYNDYFRDWY	L.R.	125	SJ 150429
GOLFA	W.L.R.	125	SJ 191066
GWERSYLLT	H.W.	117	SJ 319533
HALFWAY	G.O.T.	115	SH 772832
HALFWAY	S.M.R.	115	SH 597574
HARLECH	M.P.	124	SH 580314
HAWARDEN	H.W.	117	SJ 311658
HAWARDEN BRIDGE	H.W.	117	SJ 311695
HEBRON	S.M.R.	115	SH 583584
HENDY	T.R.	135	SH 597012
HENIARTH GATE	W.L.R.	125	SJ 123081
HOLYHEAD	C.H.	114	SH 248822
HOPE	H.W.	117	SJ 306582
LLANABER	M.P.	124	SH 598180
LLANBADARN	V.O.R.	135	SN 598806
LLANBEDR	M.P.	124	SH 579268
LLANBERIS	S.M.R.	115	SH 582597
LLANDANWG	M.P.	124	SH 570286
LLANDECWYN	M.P.	124	SH 618378
LLANDUDNO	L.B.	115	SH 784819
LLANDUDNO JUNCTION	C.H.	115	SH 795779
LLANFAIR CAEREINION	W.L.R.	125	SJ 106068
LLANFAIR P.G.	C.H.	114&115	SH 526715
LLANFAIRFECHAN	C.H.	115	SH 678751
LLANGOLLEN	L.R.	117	SJ 214421

STATION NAME	LINE	MAP No	Reference
LLANGOWER	B.L.R.	125	SH 902321
LLANRWST	L.B.	116	SH800617
LLANRWST NORTH.	L.B.	115	SH 795622
LLANUWCHLLYN	B.L.R.	125	SH 880300
LLWYNGWRIL	M.P.	124	SH 587097
MACHYNLLETH	S.A.	135	SH 744013
MINFFORDD	F.R.	124	SH 600385
MINFFORDD	M.P.	124	SH 599386
MORFA MAWDDACH	M.P.	124	SH 628141
NANT GWERNOL	T.R.	124	SH 681066
NANTYRONEN	V.O.R.	135	SN 674781
NEWTOWN	S.A.	136	SO 110912
PEN Y CHAIN	M.P.	123	SH 428365
PEN Y MOUNT HALT	W.H.P.	124	SH 571393
PENDRE	T.R.	135	SH 590008
PENHELYG	M.P.	135	SN 620961
PENMAENMAWR	C.H.	115	SH 718765
PENRHYN	F.R.	124	SH 613395
PENRHYNDEUDRAETH	M.P.	124	SH 613388
PEN-SARN	M.P.	124	SH 578279
PENTREPIOD HALT	B.L.R.	125	SH 886315
PENYBONT BALA	B.L.R.	125	SH 930350
PENYFFORDD	H.W.	117	SJ 295611
PLAS HALT	F.R.	124	SH 655407
PONT-Y-PANT	L.B.	115	SH 753535
PORTHMADOG HARBOUR	F.R.	124	SH 571384
PORTHMADOG W.H.R.	W.H.P.	124	SH 567391
PORTHMADOG	M.P.	124	SH 565392
PRESTATYN	C.H.	116	SJ 064830
PWLLHELI	M.P.	123	SH 375350
QUARRY SIDING	T.R.	124	SH 654050
RAVEN SQUARE	W.L.R.	126	SJ 216074
RHEIDOL FALLS	V.O.R.	135	SN 708787
RHIWFRON	V.O.R.	135	SN 728778
RHOSNEIGR	C.H.	114	SH 328738
RHYDYRONEN	T.R.	135	SH 614022
RHYL	C.H.	116	SJ 009812
ROMAN BRIDGE	L.B.	115	SH 713514
RUABON	C.C.	117	SJ 300438
SHOTTON	C.C. & H.W.	117	SJ 307690
SUMMIT	G.O.T.	115	SH 766833
SUMMIT	S.M.R.	115	SH 609543
SYLFAN	W.L.R.	125	SJ 176064
TAL Y CAFN	L.B.	115	SH 787717
TALSARNAU	M.P.	124	SH 610361
TAL-Y-BONT	M.P.	124	SH 586214
TAN-Y-BWLCH.	F.R.	124	SH 650415
TANYGRISIAU	F.R.	124	SH 682450
TONFANAU	M.P.	135	SH 563039
TY CROES	C.H.	114	SH 349723
TYGWYN	M.P.	124	SH 602349

STATION NAME	LINE	MAP No	Reference
TYNLLWYN HALT	T.R.	135	SH 610026
TYWYN	M.P.	135	SH 583006
VALLEY	C.H.	114	SH 292791
VICTORIA STATION	G.O.T.	115	SH 778827
WELSHPOOL	S.A.	126	SJ 229071
WHARF TYWYN	T.R.	135	SH 585004
WREXHAM CENTRAL	H.W.	117	SJ 332502
WREXHAM GENERAL	C.C.& H.W.	117	SJ 329509

OTHER ATTRACTIONS	SITE REF	MAP No	Reference
ABERYSTWYTH ELECTRIC CLIFF RAILWAY	A.C.R.	135	SN 583825
LEIN AMLWCH RAILWAY CENTRE	A.R.C.	114	SH 442927
ANGLESEY MODEL VILLAGE	A.M.V.	114	SH 434653
CENTRE FOR ALTERNATIVE TECHNOLOGY	C.A.T.	135	SH 754044
CONWY VALLEY RAILWAY MUSEUM	C.V.R.	115	SH 795565
CORRIS RAILWAY MUSEUM	C.R.M.	124	SH 755078
FAIRBOURNE & BARMOUTH STEAM RAILWAY	F.B.R.	124	SH 615128
INTERNATIONAL MODEL RAILWAY WORLD	I.M.W.	117	SJ 218420
JOYS OF LIFE COUNTRY PARK BETHESDA	J.O.L.	115	SH 619663
KIVOLI CENTRE BALA	K.C.B.	125	SH 930360
LLECHWEDD SLATE CAVERNS	L.S.C.	115	SH 699470
LLYWERNOG MINE MUSEUM	L.M.M.	135	SN 732808
MOSTYNS CAFE LLANDUDNO	M.C.	115	SH 781824
PENRHYN CASTLE MUSEUM	P.C.M.	115	SH 602710
RHYL MINIATURE RAILWAY	R.M.R.	116	SJ 000807

THANKS

I would like to thank my wife Marion for all her help in preparing this book.

I would also like to thank:

The station and train staff of North Western Trains and Central Trains for the courteous way in which they helped me.

The staff on all the narrow gauge railways, cable hauled lines and other attractions for helpful replies to questions both when I visited them and on the telephone.

The staff of the Tourist Information Centres, for supplying information on their areas, and new sites.

The staff at the Snowdonia National Park offices, for confirming details of the park boundaries.